Women and Magna Carta

Also by Jocelynne A. Scutt

RAPE LAW REFORM *(ed) (1980)*

VIOLENCE IN THE FAMILY *(ed) (1980)*

RESTORING VICTIMS OF CRIME *(1980)*

WOMEN AND CRIME *(ed, with SK Mukherjee) (1981, 2016)*

EVEN IN THE BEST OF HOMES: Violence in the Family *(1983, 1990)*

FOR RICHER, FOR POORER: Money, Marriage and Property Rights *(with Di Graham) (1984)*

POOR NATION OF THE PACIFIC: Australia's Future *(ed.)(1985)*

GROWING UP FEMINIST: The New Generation of Australian Women *(ed.)(1985)*

DIFFERENT LIVES: Reflections on the Women's Movement and Visions of Its Future *(ed.) (1987)*

LIONEL MURPHY – A Radical Judge *(ed.)(1987)*

THE BABY MACHINE: Commercialisation of Motherhood *(ed.)(1988, 1990)*

WOMEN AND THE LAW: Cases and Commentary *(1990)*

THE SEXUAL GERRYMANDER: Women and the Economics of Power *(1994)*

THE INCREDIBLE WOMAN: Power and Sexual Politics *(2 Vols)(1997)*

ESSAYS IN SPORT AND THE LAW *(ed, with T. Hickie, R. Hughes and D. Healey)(2008)*

Artemis 'Women's Voices, Women's Lives' series

BREAKING THROUGH: Women, Work and Careers *(ed.)(1992)*

AS A WOMAN: Writing Women's Lives *(ed.)(1992)*

GLORIOUS AGE: Growing Older Gloriously *(ed.)(1993)*

NO FEAR OF FLYING: Women at Home and Abroad *(ed.)(1993)*

TAKING A STAND: Women in Politics and Society *(ed.)(1994)*

CITY WOMEN, COUNTRY WOMEN: Crossing the Boundaries *(ed.)(1995)*

SINGULAR WOMEN: Reclaiming Spinsterhood *(ed.)(1995)*

LIVING GENEROUSLY: Women Mentoring Women *(ed.)(1996)*

GROWING UP FEMINIST/GROWING UP FEMINIST TOO: Raising Women, Raising Consciousness *(ed.)(1996)*

DOI: 10.1057/9781137562357.0001

palgrave▸**pivot**

Women and Magna Carta: A Treaty for Rights or Wrongs?

Jocelynne A. Scutt
University of Buckingham, UK

DOI: 10.1057/9781137562357.0001

First published 2016 by
PALGRAVE MACMILLAN

The author has asserted her right to be identified as the author of this work in accordance with the Copyright, Designs and Patents Act 1988.

Palgrave Macmillan in the UK is an imprint of Macmillan Publishers Limited, registered in England, company number 785998, of Houndmills, Basingstoke, Hampshire, RG21 6XS.

Palgrave Macmillan in the US is a division of Nature America, Inc., One New York Plaza, Suite 4500 New York, NY 10004-1562.

Palgrave Macmillan is the global academic imprint of the above companies and has companies and representatives throughout the world.

Hardback ISBN: 978-1-137-56234-0
E-PUB ISBN: 978-1-137-56236-4
E-PDF ISBN: 978-1-137-56235-7
DOI: 10.1057/9781137562357

Distribution in the UK, Europe and the rest of the world is by Palgrave Macmillan®, a division of Macmillan Publishers Limited, registered in England, company number 785998, of Houndmills, Basingstoke, Hampshire RG21 6XS.

Library of Congress Cataloging-in-Publication Data is available from the Library of Congress

A catalog record for this book is available from the Library of Congress

A catalogue record for the book is available from the British Library.

Remembering Alice Suter
Far more than just 'another' woman…
Pankhurst v Porter (1917) 23 CLR 504

DOI: 10.1057/9781137562357.0001

Contents

DOI: 10.1057/9781137562357.0001

Acknowledgements

In the writing of *Women and Magna Carta*, my good fortune has been the support of those without whom completion of this book would have been far more difficult. Thank you to, most particularly, Robin R. Joyce, and Felicity Beth Gaulard, Kerry Heubel, Karen Buczynski-Lee, Patmalar Ambikapathy Thuraisingham, Bob McMullan, Susan Edwards, Anne Mitchell and Ian Fryatt.

▶

palgrave▸**pivot**

www.palgrave.com/pivot

1
Introduction – Magna Carta: Women's Rights or Wrongs?

Abstract: *In 2015 Magna Carta turned 800. A treaty between king and barons, today Magna Carta is claimed as a fundamental statement of rights. No woman was at Runnymede. Women appear in Magna Carta as attached to men – widows and daughters. So, asks Scutt, does Magna Carta speak for women? Some women spoke independently in medieval Britain, although church and aristocracy circumscribed all women's sphere. Little is written of women and Magna Carta historically or in women's rights campaigns. Mary Wollstonecraft demanded rights, and some campaigns reflect Magna Carta's terms without invoking them directly. For men, Magna Carta is 'adaptable', a 'speaking statute' encompassing new rights and supporting contemporary claims. Scutt asks if Magna Carta thus promotes women's rights, or does it symbolise wrongs done to women?*

Keywords: Magna Carta a 'speaking' statute; Magna Carta 'adaptable'; Magna Carta's impact on women; no women in Magna Carta; sexual prejudice; women and Magna Carta rights

Scutt, Jocelynne A. *Women and Magna Carta: A Treaty for Rights or Wrongs?* Basingstoke: Palgrave Macmillan, 2016. DOI: 10.1057/9781137562357.0003.

> John by the grace of God, king of England, lord of Ireland, duke
> of Normandy and Aquitaine, count of Anjou, to his archbishops,
> bishops, abbots, earls, barons, justices, foresters, sheriffs, reeves,
> ministers and all his bailiffs and faithful men, greeting ...
>
> *Magna Carta 1215*

Magna Carta initiated

Magna Carta is generally seen as a statement of rights. A treaty between
king and barons, its provisions often claim to extend rights and freedoms
to 'ordinary' British subjects. When agreed at Runnymede in 1215,
neither barons nor king had any concept of 'equal rights for all' (beyond
themselves); there was no desire to include the masses. The barons'
intentions were twofold. Magna Carta was designed to curb King John's
excesses towards them and theirs: clauses limited his power to extract
taxes and other emoluments, reduced his prerogative to determine
when and whom wards and widows might marry, and denied his right
to assert untrammelled power over rivers and royal forests. Equally or
more significantly, the treaty established a council of twenty-five, chosen
by and from the barons, to ensure the king's compliance. The Council
of Barons would 'with all their might ... observe, maintain and cause to
be observed' the 'peace and liberties' confirmed and granted by Magna
Carta, while 'anyone in the realm' could 'take an oath to obey the orders
of the twenty-five barons' in enforcing it.[1]

At its heart, Magna Carta meant that the monarch could no longer
exercise independent and complete power. Rather, King John (and, as
intended, his successors) would be obliged not only to comply with its
provisions, but to follow the barons' interpretation of them, submitting
to their final 'say' on whether or not he strayed or disobeyed. The king
would not be above the law.

It was not as if kings had never sealed agreements with nobles before.
John's father, King Henry II, did so. Yet there was no suggestion that
Henry ruled at their behest. As it was, John was never expected to
rule. Of Henry and Eleanor of Aquitaine's eight children, William died
early, leaving next-in-line Henry as heir. Henry died just short of thirty.
Matilda, being a woman, was automatically 'out'. Next, Geoffrey died, so
upon Henry II's demise, in 1189, Richard succeeded him. Ten years on,
Richard's unexpected death meant John reigned.

DOI: 10.1057/9781137562357.0003

'John the Tyrant' generated such unrest, bitterness and resentment that barons rebelled. Albeit successful in securing his seal to Magna Carta, they mistrusted his readiness to comply. Indeed, a king should not be a law unto himself. Henry II, Richard I, and fifteen years of John's rule precipitated the barons into thoughts of shared control. Thoughts transformed into action. The twenty-five would serve as a permanent imperial 'directorate'. All twenty-five were men.

In Magna Carta, not a single woman's name appears. Women are mentioned, but through their relationships with men, as with heiresses, wards or widows, and the Scots' king's daughters – John's hostages. Women were classified by affiliated or sexual status. As Henrietta Leyser's *Medieval Women* notes, men could be considered collectively 'as knights, merchants, crusaders'. Women were 'virgins, wives or widows [and] mothers'.[2] None was an archbishop, bishop, abbot, earl, baron, justice, forester, sheriff, reeve, minister, bailiff or 'faithful man'. Although, as Louise Wilkinson recounts in *Women as Sheriffs*, on 18 October 1216 John appointed a woman, Lady Nicholaa de la Haye (c.1169–1230), as joint sheriff (with a man) of Lincolnshire and 'worthy ... of God's protection "in body and soul"', she played no part in Magna Carta. Nor did any other woman.

No woman signed. Yet women were not entirely lacking status. Nor were they voiceless. In the *Time Traveller's Guide*, Ian Mortimer reflects upon 'high-status females [being] just as highly respected as high-status males' (at least, by underlings). Two centuries after Magna Carta, Margery Kempe's autobiography appeared. A century before, Hildegard of Bingen preached throughout Europe, travelling from Paris to Switzerland, to southern Germany, back to France and around once more. Clamorous listeners requested written versions of her orations. Her commanding remonstrations had the interdict against her convent removed. She wrote to popes, bishops, nuns, emperors and nobility. Her works comprised hundreds of letters, songs, poems, books – including discourses on herbal remedies and the human body, a commentary on the Gospels and one on the Athanasian Creed, and a play set to music, the *Ordo Virtutum*. She exchanged letters with her friend and rival, Elizabeth of Shonau, who authored three books of *Visions* (two, perhaps, with her brother Egbert) and *Liber viarum Die*, enjoining the clergy and the laity, wed and unwed, to live lives of piety and holiness, without hypocrisy or cant.[3]

Yet class did not inhibit sexual prejudice. Mortimer's *Time Traveller's Guide* records the medieval convention of holding women responsible

DOI: 10.1057/9781137562357.0003

for 'all physical, intellectual and moral weaknesses of society'. A contradictory mixture of traits and physical attributes asserted that women were 'smaller, meeker, more demure, more gentle, more supple and more delicate', simultaneously being 'more envious and more laughing and loving', while the souls of women housed malice, more so than men's. Besides, it was said, women exceeded men in mendacity and feebleness of nature, always working in a more tardy fashion and moving at a pace slower than a man.[4] In light of this bigotry, it is little wonder that women were absent from Magna Carta's drafting, negotiation, sealing or execution.

In *Magna Carta*, JC Holt denotes 'adaptability' as Magna Carta's 'greatest and most important characteristic'. Part of its potential, he concludes, is an interpretation giving it 'qualities which the men (sic) of 1215 did not intend'.[5] Does this mean Magna Carta supported women claiming legal rights, protections and status, or it could advance them? Do women's claims 'fit' and – if extending to women –

‣ what provisions apply directly to women and how do they treat women: to be controlled, or entitled to rights and freedoms?

‣ what provisions make no reference to women – yet might extend rights and freedoms to women?

Does Magna Carta advance women's rights, or is it a recipe for controlling women, perpetuating domination rather than liberation?

Magna Carta, women, law and history

Some six centuries after Runnymede, Magna Carta's exhortations for freemen's rights resonated with Mary Wollstonecraft and her contemporary, American Joel Barlow:

> The word 'liberty' ... would not have been known in any language, had people not felt deprived of it; and some are 'free men' because 'men are not all free'.[6]

As Wollstonecraft expostulated in 1792, neither were women 'all free'. Hence, her proclamation in *A Vindication of the Rights of Woman*, building on and generating centuries of women's struggle for freedom, for rights as freewomen, and for freedom as persons. Resonating beyond the UK and US, Wollstonecraft became a rallying cry for women throughout the Empire and then the Commonwealth. Women from Canada, Australia

DOI: 10.1057/9781137562357.0003

and Aotearoa/New Zealand initiated their own struggles, interacting across oceans, and across national boundaries.

As Chapter 2, 'Are Women Persons', recounts, the failure to acknowledge women as identities in their own right permeates actual history, the writing of history and the recognition that women might make and record history too. Over centuries, women have recorded their own lives and the lives of other women, yet male treatises and men's histories are more often published and remembered. Women's works come to attention, then fade, are sometimes recovered, or new generations of women write 'herstory' all over again. What of women and Magna Carta?

Unearthing women writing of women's worlds and works at the time of John, Runnymede, Magna Carta and the rebellion's impact on them is not so easy. Histories are there – Judith M. Bennett and Ruth Mazo Karras with *The Oxford Handbook of Women and Gender* (2013), Vicki Leon's *Outrageous Women* (1998), and Marcelle Theibaux's collection, *The Writings of Medieval Women* (1994) – showing women did and could write 'then'. Magna Carta features by its very absence, yet historians' concentration on men's involvement and its impact on men may be unremarkable, for Eileen Power's 1920s work on *Medieval Women* and *Medieval English Nunneries* recognises women moved within a circumscribed sphere – if women moved at all:

...the ideas about women were formed on the one hand by the clerkly order [the Church], usually celibate, and on the other hand by a narrow caste [the aristocracy], who could afford to regard its women as an ornamental asset, while strictly subordinating them to the interests of its primary asset, the land...[T]he accepted theory about the nature and sphere of women was the work of the classes least familiar with the great mass of womankind.[7]

Whether highborn or lowborn, women lived under the direction of fathers, husbands, or church. Although young men were subject to their father's will, those highborn being deployed in marriage to make alliances and increase a family's wealth and status, unlike young women they were not perennial 'non-persons'. Once reaching their age of majority, sons gained a preeminent place in their own household or that prospect lay before them. For a woman, whatever her age, personhood was beyond her realm.

As for treatises reflecting law and legal history, that Magna Carta might be significant for women's liberty was not within contemplation of jurists Bracton (c.1210–c.1268), Coke (1552–1634), Hale (1609–1676),

DOI: 10.1057/9781137562357.0003

and Blackstone (1723–1789). Nor did Glanville (1112–1190), John's tutor and chief minister of England during Henry II's reign, anticipate it. In London in 1854, Barbara Leigh-Smith Bodichon published her *Laws of England Concerning Women*, then in 1894 Charlotte Carmichael Stopes' *British Freewomen* appeared, claiming Magna Carta's language for women, whatever judges might say. In the US, Elizabeth Cady Stanton's *Women's Bible*, Parts I (1895) and II (1898), reflected the law's failure to acknowledge women's 'whole' identity and religion's undermining of it. However not until 750 years after Magna Carta did Albie Sachs and Joan Hoff Wilson's ground-breaking work appear, analysing women's lack of personhood in US and UK law. *Sexism and the Law*, published in 1978, confronted deftly the judicial guile (perhaps cunning) producing the jurisprudential nonsense deeming women as 'non-persons'. Sachs and Wilson exposed this excuse for women's absence from bench and bar, parliament and professorships for what it was: a manufactured reason for legitimating women's absence when truth was, bluntly, that (too many) men did not want women there. Magna Carta won no mention. Nor did it when, almost fifty years on, Robert J. Sharpe and Patricia I. McMahon in *The Persons Case* (2007) once more addressed the law's women-are-not-persons conundrum.

From 1759 to 1797, Wollstonecraft lived and died, for years judged wanton and wanting. A creative woman and 'new genus' she, like her medieval sisters, was scorned by unreasoned and unreasoning opinion dripping in sexual prejudice. Yet as Chapter 3, 'Are Women Peers', relates, Magna Carta called for judgement by peers, transmuting into today's jury. Would women's campaign for adjudication in courtrooms vindicate Wollstonecraft or condemn her? Historical and jurisprudentially based work effectively addresses this question. Citing the Bill of Rights 6th Amendment, based on Magna Carta, Holly J. McCammon's treatise, *The U.S. Women's Jury Movements*, focuses on archival material reflecting 19th- and 20th-century campaigns. In the UK, Australia, Canada and Aotearoa/New Zealand, academic and practising lawyers have researched juries, though little explicitly directed to women's role. If mentioned, Magna Carta is not centre stage. Focusing on minorities, following an earlier 'all white juries' study with no Magna Carta backdrop, in 2010, Cheryl Thomas conducted a major review *Are juries fair?* for the UK Ministry of Justice. Neil Vidmar's *World Jury Systems* (2004) and, with Valerie Hans, *Judging the Jury* (1986) look at similarities and differences – the latter, principally Canada and the US, the former reviewing amongst

DOI: 10.1057/9781137562357.0003

others England, the US, Australia, Aotearoa/New Zealand, Canada, Scotland and Ireland (NI and Republic). They contain references to women, but nothing headed 'Women and Juries', 'Women as Jurors' or 'Magna Carta'. Vidmar and Regina Schuller's 'The Canadian Criminal Jury' (2011) acknowledges Britain as originator, but again, Magna Carta's absence is replicated by a paucity of reference to women. Neil Cameron, Susan Potter and Warren Young recognise colonial history and English heritage in 'The New Zealand Jury' – but nothing on Magna Carta and little on women. Michael Chesterman's 1997 article explores juries and 'sensationalist' or sensationalised crimes involving women – as accused (Alice Lynne Chamberlain in Australia's 'dingo's got my baby' case) and as victim (OJ Simpson and the death of Nicole Simpson and her friend Ronald Goldman), while Kate Auty and Sandy Toussaint's *A Jury of Whose Peers?* (2004) carries entire chapters on women and juries, analysing their impact and socio-cultural meanings. Still, no Magna Carta.

Addressing land rights in the late 15th century, Margery Paston and, her mother-in-law, Margaret Paston sought support from Norfolk's dowager duchess in John Paston's property dispute. Articulate and forceful, consistent with Magna Carta they nonetheless saw their delegation as regaining or retaining 'his' land. Leyser's *Medieval Women* refers briefly to Magna Carta in this context: widows 'effectively denied ... any choice at all', because property rights were male. Women's status dictated inheritance 'rights', exemplified by the 1185 *Register of Rich Widows and of Orphaned Heirs and Heiresses* – a list of those 'in the king's gift', women and property employed by kings as bargaining tools for enhancing regional power. Amy Louise Erickson follows with *Women and Property in Early Modern England* (1993) and, addressing Victorian women's lives and legal status, Joan Perkin's *Women and Marriage* (1989) and *Victorian Women* (1995) reveal women's efforts to avoid legal and historical oppression centred in property rights (for men) and wrongs (for women). Marylynn Salmon's *Women and the Law of Property* (1986) addresses US women's property rights history. For Canada, Anne Lorene Chambers' *Married Women and Property Law* (1997) combines law past and present, as do Angela Barns, Andrew Cowie and Therese Jefferson in *Women's Property Rights* (2009) for Australia, while Maureen Baker provides historical and sociological insights for Aotearoa/New Zealand, Canada and Australia in *Families, Labour and Love* (2001). Magna Carta being implicit, not explicit in this scholarship, Chapter 4 'Can Women Be Householders?' draws together women's struggles arising out of Magna Carta, detailing

DOI: 10.1057/9781137562357.0003

its limited gestures towards widows and property, and recounting the still unfinished fight for women's claims.

Similarly with legal wrangles, Chapter 5 'Access to Law and Justice' addresses women's rights in civil disputes and ongoing demand for remedies. Critically, Magna Carta focused on access to law and the rights of the governed (the barons) to challenge the governor (the king). Holt points out that the Angevin kings developed a stable adjudication system for freemen in disputes with their lords, but no such system for barons vis-à-vis their lord, the king.[8] The barons sought a reliable system, not one predicated on John's inconstancy. The medieval court followed the king. Henry II travelled out of London – sometimes. Richard went north rarely. John travelled to Nottingham, Lincoln, Derby, Oxford, Bedford and Buckinghamshire, Wallingford, Norfolk, Norwich, and points beyond and between. The barons stood disconcerted. When having their cases heard, they wanted them heard in one place. Though the king might want to travel around and about, they did not – with little or no notice, and much added expense. That women might be similarly disconcerted by peripatetic dispute settlement was not in barons' minds nor Magna Carta's lines. Holt and others confirm instances of women in property disputes, some apparently bringing cases in their own name (most with a male relative).[9] But that women as freewomen might have legal standing – the right to sue – was not in prospect. That women as freewomen might wish to challenge government decisions (the king) was beyond the realms of Magna Carta reality. Centuries on, in *Sex, Power and Justice* (1995), Greta Bird and Diane Kirkby explore indigenous, non-indigenous and 'ethnic-background' women's legal system experience over 200 years of colonised history, with Aotearoa/New Zealand and Australian Commissions recounting obstacles to justice and opportunities for access: *Women's Access to Legal Services* (1999), *Women and Access to Justice* (1995–1999) and *Equality Before the Law* (1994). Similarly the Canadian Advisory Council on the Status of Women analysed *Canadian Charter Equality Rights for Women* (1989), and Canada's LEAF researches and promotes legal services and access for women, as in Alison Brewin's *Legal Aid Denied* (1994). In the US, states and independent agencies produce reports, and scholars publish on women's (lack of) access rights in historical (Felice Batlan, 2015) and contemporary (Deborah L. Rhode, 2002) perspective, while in Britain, amongst others, the Fawcett Society and Rights of Women (2002) pursue civil interventions for women, consistent with Magna Carta's refrain of rights to law and justice.

DOI: 10.1057/9781137562357.0003

For revenue and the franchise, Chapter 6, 'No Taxation without Representation', explores women's campaign for a say in the polity and the raising of revenue, Magna Carta's affirmation for barons and freemen. Just as men's voices must be heeded, women's voices demand a hearing. Here, women's enfranchisement has a high history profile, less so women's tax status. Women's populist movements in Britain, North America, Aotearoa/New Zealand and Australia echoed Magna Carta's 'no taxation' refrain in an egalitarian voice. Only now is scholarship beginning to catch up. Building on Harriet Martineau (1802–1876), led by Patricia Apps' tax analysis in her 1981 *A Theory of Inequality*, added to by Marilyn Waring's work on women and economics, *If Women Counted* (1988), and followed by Ann Mumford's 2010 comparative law perspective, *Tax Policy, Women and the Law*, the inequities of women's tax liability, (under)valuing of 'women's work', and role of global finance are dissected with precision. In declaring 'no taxation without the common counsel of the realm', Magna Carta recognised that without representation, tax inequities and iniquities follow. So women demand equality in 'the realm's common counsel', to end tax and wage inequities and iniquities.

Medieval women's bodies were not their own. They gained no Magna Carta mention. Woman-as-chattel did. In *The Medieval Vagina* (2014), Karen Harris and Lori Caskey-Sigety traverse the charge that women, not being men, are 'inferior', their bodies 'somehow unnatural'. Women past, like women present, resisted wanton use and abuse of women's bodies and lack of bodily integrity. In 1975, Susan Brownmiller's *Against Our Will* prompted global adoption of the chant 'yes means yes, no means no ...'. Erin Pizzey's *Scream Quietly* (1979) and Jocelynne Scutt's *Even in the Best of Homes* (1983) took the message 'women's bodies count' into UK and Australian homes and beyond, with Andrea Dworkin's (1981, 1997) oeuvre extending the debating lines. Yet women are bound by more than the body construct. Real bonds grow out of physiology and meanings imposed upon biology, as Simone De Beauvoir provocatively decreed in *The Second Sex* (1953) and Germaine Greer in *The Female Eunuch* (1979), building on those before them and providing followers a platform. Law binds women just as strongly. For the US, Catharine Mackinnon's (1989, 2007) work exemplifies this, while Helena Kennedy (1993) and Susan Edwards' (1981, 2013) UK work, Mary Jane Mossman's (1996, 2006) Canadian scholarship, Australia's Scutt (1990, 1996), Margaret Thornton (1996), Regina Graycar and Jenny Morgan (2002), and Aotearoa/New Zealand scholars expand the lines. Making Magna Carta meaningful,

DOI: 10.1057/9781137562357.0003

Chapter 7, 'Bring Up the Bodies', relates women's struggle to be free from the strictures binding women's bodies to their husbands and in-laws, a central claim in the pantheon of claims for women's right to be human.

When Magna Carta decreed that no one should be imprisoned without due process of law, could a woman call on habeas corpus if imprisoned by her husband? This leads to the fundamental question in Chapter 8 'Conclusion – Claiming Magna Carta Rights' namely, the implications of this 800-year-old event for women's rights and freedoms. Did women's absence from the text and the scene of sealing Magna Carta mean women not only had no voice then, but could claim no justice now? Traversing today's renewed demand by US women for an Equal Rights Amendment (ERA), this chapter acknowledges the activism of women of the west, when women of Australian and US western states made the earliest gains. It recognises, too, that race and ethnicity denied women of minority background rights their brothers gained before them, just as 'white' men were privileged over their wives, widows and daughters under Magna Carta and far beyond. Yet women of all backgrounds, race/ethnicity and class have fought for rights and recognition always. This struggle is not over, yet surely after 800 years women may call on Magna Carta to conclude it.

Magna Carta – rights, wrongs and women

Magna Carta's 800th anniversary prompted efforts to 'write women in': Louise Wilkinson's scholarship in recovering John's daughter, Joan, whom he married to Llywelyn of Wales; Isabella of Gloucester, John's first wife, and Isabella of Angouleme, his second; Margaret of Scotland, John's hostage; and Jessica Nelson's recognising Isabella, countess of Norfolk (younger sister of Margaret and hostage, too), provide pictures of women who, neither ciphers nor sycophants, were courageous and bold. Yet any brave defiance was just that: constructed by and against the reality of women rating second, if at all. Whatever their deeds or derring-do, their diplomacy, debating skills or denunciation of conformity to roles of wife, daughter, mother … they were not equal, nor equals. Did they hope for Magna Carta's help?

Mid-20th century, Mary Ritter Beard recovered women, too. In *Woman as Force in History* (1946) she reconstituted women's history to affirm an agency and aptitude conventional history ignored. Affirming women

DOI: 10.1057/9781137562357.0003

who defied restrictions and restraints of legal strictures, social mores and cultural limits, she followed women who had made the argument before. One such, Harriet Taylor (1807–1858), lived with that defiance, rejecting notions that she, a married woman, should share no working intimate relationship with another man. Unlike Wollstonecraft before her, she survived opprobrium or suffered it less: her husband's acceptance of the alliance and John Stuart Mill's affirmation of her intellect no doubt tempered scorn or stopped it at its source.

Published in 1851, Taylor's *Enfranchisement of Women* attests to the strength of Magna Carta's ideas and their impact beyond John, the barons and Runnymede. Referencing the *New York Tribune*, Taylor extolled American women's organised agitation on a 'new question', observing that it was not 'new' to 'thinkers' and nor indeed:

> ... to anyone by whom the principles of free and popular government are felt as well as acknowledged, but new, and even unheard-of, as a subject for public meetings and practical political action.[10]

The question? Women's enfranchisement and 'admission, in law and in fact, to equality in all rights, political, civil, and social, with ... male citizens ...'. The 1850 Women's Rights Convention was her touchstone, 'above a thousand persons ... present throughout', and, with a larger venue, 'many thousands more would have attended'. Like the 1848 Seneca Falls Convention (of which Taylor had heard nothing), the Declaration incorporated Magna Carta sentiments:

> *Resolved* – That every human being, of full age, and resident for a proper length of time on the soil of the nation, who is required to obey the law, is entitled to a voice in its enactment; that every such person, whose property or labour is taxed for the support of the government, is entitled to a direct share in such governmental; ...

Further, women's entitlement to 'the right of suffrage, and ... eligibl[ity] to office ... [with] equality before the law, without distinction of sex or colour' must emblazon banners of all parties claiming to 'represent the humanity, the civilization, and the progress of the age ...'. More, '... civil and political rights acknowledg[ing] no sex, ... the word 'male' should be struck from every State Constitution ...'.

Yet Taylor's confidence that 'man' would not be limited to the male sex when women proclaimed the self-evident truth, that all men are created equal and endowed with inalienable rights, was misplaced. The struggle was not over, women's non-personhood was an obstacle to their claims.

DOI: 10.1057/9781137562357.0003

So, more than 150 years after Taylor's hopes, 800 years after John agreed at Runnymede under the eyes of barons intent on advancing their rights, is Magna Carta relevant to today's women? In 'Magna Carta in the Twentieth and Twenty First Centuries' (2015), Michael Beloff avers Magna Carta's role as 'an always speaking statute': it 'should be given its current, not simply its historic meaning'.[11] How then does Magna Carta in its past and current meanings speak for women? Taking Holt's applause for its adaptability, is Magna Carta a charter for advancing women's rights or a licence for affirming women's wrongs?

Notes

1   Magna Carta, cap. 61.
2   Leyser, *Medieval Women*, 1995, p. 93.
3   Mortimer, *The Time Traveller's Guide*, 2009, p. 53.
4   Mortimer, *The Time Traveller's Guide*, 2009, p. 55.
5   Holt, *Magna Carta*, 2015, p. 39.
6   Barlow, *Advice*, 1792.
7   Power, *Medieval Women*, 1995, p. 1.
8   Holt, *Magna Carta*, 2015, p. 154.
9   Holt, *Magna Carta*, 2015, pp. 130, 135.
10 Taylor Mill, 'Enfranchisement', 1851; following quotations are from that source.
11 Beloff, 'Magna Carta', 2015, p. 6.

DOI: 10.1057/9781137562357.0003

2
Are Women Persons?

Abstract: *Some medieval women exercised independence, although church and aristocracy dictated women's role. Christine de Pizan and Wollstonecraft resisted while Blackstone said women benefited from English laws denying them rights. Women's campaigns for public office, enfranchisement, entering university or practicing professions encountered judges labelling women 'non-persons', denying them rights that men claimed as their entitlement. Scutt describes Australian, Aotearoa/New Zealand, UK and US women confronting such judicial nonsense. Susan B. Anthony, Sophia Jex-Blake and women like them hammered at the doors of all-male courts for recognition as persons, or implored all-male legislatures for Acts granting 'women' rights. Canadian women won the breakthrough when the Privy Council recognised them as persons. Yet even today, abortion laws and surrogacy still cast women into a subhuman sphere, denying women full personhood.*

Keywords: abortion rights; are women persons?; surrogacy as denying women agency; women and education; women and professions; women and university; women's agency; women's bodily integrity; women's (lack of) personhood; women's rights campaigns

Scutt, Jocelynne A. *Women and Magna Carta: A Treaty for Rights or Wrongs?* Basingstoke: Palgrave Macmillan, 2016. DOI: 10.1057/9781137562357.0004.

> We have ... granted to all freemen of our kingdom, for us and our heirs forever, all the underwritten liberties, to be had and held by them and their heirs, of us and our heirs forever.
>
> *Magna Carta, cap. 1*

Does 'man' embrace 'woman'?

In 1850, the UK Parliament passed 'An Act for shortening the Language used in Acts of Parliament'. Under Lord Brougham's Act, 'unless expressly provided to the contrary', words importing the masculine gender would be 'deemed and taken to include female'. Today, some Interpretation Acts endorse gender-neutral language in statutes. Some continue the legislative fiction where 'man embraces woman'.

Magna Carta incorporates no such fiction. 'Freeman' did not mean 'freewoman'. *Black's Law Dictionary* defines 'freemen' as men possessing and enjoying all civil and political rights under a free government. Some men were excluded from king's grant under Magna Carta. Slaves, vassals or villeins did not count (although villeins at least gained amercement – fines or penalties – relief). Yet consistent with Holt's notion of Magna Carta's 'adaptability' and Beloff's 'always speaking' principle, time saw Magna Carta become socially inclusive. Under Edward III, 'freeman' became 'man' (1321, 1352), then 'man of whatever estate or condition he may be' (1354). By 1628, Coke's *Second Institute* asserted that 'due process' extended to villeins.[1] How did women fare?

In 1215, the church was central to social and cultural life. Common law and ecclesiastical law coexisted. Ecclesiastical law impacted on women's religious and secular lives. Religious precepts elevating men as head of household and family did not end on the church stoop, prevailing inside and outside the home. Meanwhile, 'benefit of clergy', the common law provision enabling escape from the death penalty for felonies, benefitted men alone. A man who could read a nominated scripture (possibly learned by heart) dodged the gallows. Because the church rejected women as clerics, literate women, or women capable of memorising text, lost protection of pretence or fiction of being clergy: they could not escape hanging.

Through the medieval period, some women exercised some civil and political rights. On occasion a woman, particularly widows whose husbands had held substantial lands, voted in parliamentary elections. Sometimes widows entered trades by taking over their husband's bakery,

DOI: 10.1057/9781137562357.0004

foundry or blacksmithy. Some ran their own businesses. Some appeared as courtroom litigants when their livelihood or lands were threatened. Yet widows are warned against going to law unless lacking alternatives. Outlining ways of avoiding the courts through courtesy or making 'every reasonable offer to settle', in *The Treasure of the City of Ladies*, published in 1405, Christine De Pizan recommends steps if legal action is inescapable. First, seek lawyers' advice; secondly, pursue the case with 'great care and diligence'; thirdly, have money. Ignore these and, whatever the strength of her case, a widow is 'in danger of losing it'.[2]

Pizan's works crossed the English Channel. Her son served in an English aristocratic household; she was invited to join Henry IV's court which she refused; then, almost a century later, Henry VIII had *The Book of Feats of Arms and Chivalry*, her practical treatise on running an army, translated and published for his troops.[3] Although *The Treasure* addresses French civil law, differing from common law England, women – French or English – were vulnerable in a world where they generally lacked authority or public power.

Lacking rights and privileges that freemen had did not excuse women from socio-political and economic burdens. A woman might escape criminal responsibility by pleading that she acted under coercion when committing a crime, other than treason or murder, in her husband's presence. Yet this concession was isolated, dependent upon a wife's inferior status. Marriage denied a woman the personhood she might otherwise enjoy. 'Coverture' made husband and wife one – that 'one' being the husband. Wives gave up identity, person, property and income to their husband's ownership. Without her husband's concurrence, a wife was denied the right to seek compensation for injuries she suffered – any action must be brought in his name. A wife was entitled to her husband's upkeep – for necessaries only; if she managed to buy on credit, her husband was liable only for goods required for simple sustenance. Legally a man could keep his wife in penury. If she killed him, the 1351 Treason Act made her guilty of petty treason, subject to being burnt at the stake.

Some four centuries later, in referring to coverture, jurist William Blackstone saw this person-less state as advantaging women. Having outlined the limitations of wifehood, his 1765 *Commentaries on the Laws of England* asserted:

> [E]ven the disabilities which the wife lies under are for the most part intended for her protection and benefit: so great a favourite is the female sex of the laws of England.[4]

DOI: 10.1057/9781137562357.0004

Single women were not much better off. As in Magna Carta's time, despite some exceptions for adult single women, they generally lived under their father's control until marriage. This applied across the classes, giving young women little latitude for exercising any rights they might have. Those meaning single might go into a nunnery where, Pizan's 1405 treatise stressed, seven principal virtues prevailed: obedience, humility, sobriety, patience, solicitude, chastity, and concord and benevolence.[5] Single women assuming independence were eventually controlled. The Beguines, collectives of single or widowed women living in European communities or communes, serving the poor independent of the church, eventually died, were disbanded or moved into religious orders. Walter Simons' *Cities of Ladies* records their flourishing from 1200 to 1565. Living in 'beguinages' in cities and towns, they offended openly against notions of a woman's place. Laura Swan in *The Wisdom of the Beguines* describes them as a women's movement, at a time when the church dictated how women should live and be. Beguines did not marry. Nor did they want to. Yet operating outside the strictures of religious orders was seen as defiance. To the church, their very existence was threatening, their mode of living heretical.

In *Medieval Women*, Leyser reflects on the elusive nature of a history of English women in establishing collectives like the Beguines, yet spinsters displayed considerable spirited independence.[6] Earning their own income at the spinning wheel, they actively denounced the sale of wives by disgruntled or avaricious husbands. Swooping down on market day when 'wife sales' were advertised, spinsters disrupted the husband or auctioneer in his sales pitch, often enabling women to escape, shaming husbands into giving up, or driving away prospective purchasers. Predictably, their status was undermined, the meaning of 'spinster' becoming distorted. No longer identified as independent, income-earning women with rebellion on their minds and women's rights activism in their blood, they were demoted as ashamed, sad and bitter unwed women.[7] Class didn't help. Those with brothers became household help or governesses. Some became governesses in other families' households or seamstresses or mantua makers. An unmarried older woman's life was not easy, her dependence on charitable parish or relatives was almost inevitable. Yet despite Magna Carta's 'adaptability', 'freeman' was not transmuted by Edward III into 'woman of whatever estate or condition she may be'.

Single women or 'girls and older women in the state of virginity' rate an entire chapter in *The Treasure*, with Pizan asserting demeanour as their

DOI: 10.1057/9781137562357.0004

key to a 'proper' life. They 'ought to be in their countenances, conduct and speech moderate and chaste ...', in church maintaining a quiet manner, gazing at their hymn books or sitting immobile, with lowered eyes. In the street or otherwise in public, their deportment should be 'mild and sedate'. At home idleness was forbidden: they 'must be busy always with some housework'. Pizan's rules for clothing, hair, speech and dancing were always to be demure, a single woman's best place being with her mother or in an older woman's company. Upon ageing, she played this role to young women in the state of virginity. Meanwhile, working-class girls might have some latitude in deportment, yet they, like their so-called betters, had no more rights. Nor did Edward III contemplate their being included in Magna Carta's clauses.

The Person Cases – Mark 1

Blackstone's assertion of women's advantage through being denied rights was not universal. In *A Vindication of the Rights of Woman* (1792), Wollstonecraft was far from sanguine:

> The laws respecting women ... make an absurd unit of a man and his wife; and then, by the easy transition of only considering him as responsible, she is reduced to a mere cipher.[8]

Editing *Blackstone's Commentaries* in 1793, Edward Christian agreed:

> I fear there is little reason to pay a compliment to our laws for their respect and favour to the female sex.[9]

Yet dispelling married women's non-entity status was not so easy. Unmarried women were affected, too. Courts said that not being 'persons', women should be denied men's rights and freedoms. Yet rights and freedoms 'were' Magna Carta. Wanting clear rules and a right to make them, barons sought to make their claims law by imposing their collective will upon John. Holt observes that by the 14th century, both aims had been (partially) achieved: Parliament made law through statute, and Acts of Parliament incorporated charter phrases.[10] Yet women were not in Parliament making laws, nor outside it choosing lawmakers. Whatever Magna Carta's 'adaptability', it did not speak for women.

In 1872, Susan B. Anthony voted in US federal elections. Implicitly drawing upon Magna Carta, which drafters of the US Constitution saw as a

DOI: 10.1057/9781137562357.0004

major constitutional document, Anthony relied upon the 14th Amendment. Passed by Congress and ratified in 1866, the Amendment says:

> All persons born or naturalized in the United States and subject to [its] jurisdiction..., are citizens of the United States and [their home] State... No State shall make or enforce any law [abridging] the privileges or immunities of citizens...; nor shall any State deprive any person of life, liberty, or property, without due process of law; nor deny to any person within its jurisdiction the equal protection of the laws.

Anthony, her three sisters and some fifty other women asserted registration and voting rights as citizens entitled to equal protection. Rejected, Anthony reportedly threatened to 'bring charges', suing Rochester registrars 'for large, exemplary damages!'[11] Concerned at this prospect and after 'a full hour' of discussion, registrars acceded to Anthony's demand. Next day, the *Rochester Union and Advertiser* editorial protested that citizenship conveyed the right to vote 'no more than it carries the power to fly to the moon', demanding that registered women attempting to vote should be challenged and prosecuted 'to the full extent of the law'.

Anthony and several allies voted. As prime mover, she was arrested and prosecuted. In 1873, a grand jury returned an indictment that she 'knowingly, wrongfully, and unlawfully' voted in a congressional election, despite lacking any lawful right for she was 'then and there a person of the female sex'. Awaiting trial, Anthony embarked on a lecture tour proclaiming her voting rights as a citizen and, as a person, her entitlement to the law's equal protection.

When tried, deemed 'not a competent witness on her own behalf', Anthony was denied the right to give evidence. In his concluding address Henry Seldon, her lawyer, declared that had Anthony's brother voted under the same circumstances, his act would have been recognised as 'innocent, ... honourable and laudable'. Anthony was prosecuted simply for being a woman:

> The crime therefore consists not in the act done, but in the simple fact that the person doing it was a woman and not a man. [T]his is the first instance in which a woman has been arraigned in a criminal court, merely on account of her sex...

Found guilty, Anthony took the opportunity to speak, asserting 'every vital principal... of government [was] trampled underfoot':

> My natural rights, my civil rights, my political rights, my judicial rights, are all alike ignored. Robbed of the fundamental privilege of citizenship, I am degraded from the status of a citizen to that of a subject...

DOI: 10.1057/9781137562357.0004

Not only she, but 'all [her] sex' were 'doomed to political subjection under this so-called form of government ...'. Her eloquence met with a $100 fine plus costs. She refused to pay. No doubt fearing imprisonment would provide her further political capital, the authorities forbore to demand it.

Meanwhile in Britain, more than 100 years before Anthony's trial, Sarah Bly's election as sexton of St Botolph's parish was challenged. Bly gained 169 undisputed (men's) votes plus forty from women claiming voting rights as housekeepers paying to the church and poor; her opponent Mr Olive gained 174 undisputed votes, with twenty-two such 'other' votes. In 1738, *Olive v. Ingram* presented two questions: first, whether a woman could take the office of sexton and, secondly, whether women were entitled to vote.

Not all judges demoted women into the ranks of the utterly incapable. Lee, CJ whilst ultimately deciding the case turned on its own facts and 'could not be [a] precedent', adjourned the hearing several times for further argument and deliberation.[12] During submissions, he declared the question was 'whether a woman is to be taken within the general words of "all persons paying scot and lot"', noting earlier cases confirming a Lady Packington as a returning officer, returning two members to Parliament to serve in her name, whilst *Catharine v. Surry* and *Holt v. Lyle* (1607) confirmed a single woman was qualified as freeholder to vote for members of Parliament; once married, her husband voted in her place. Nonetheless Bly's success – her election and the women's votes were deemed valid – was based on categorising the post of sexton as a trust, hence a private, not a public, office. This distinction meant women could vote for and hold the office, but on being 'incompetent' or 'incapacitated' could not stand or vote for public office. *Olive v. Ingram*'s ultimate tenor was to confirm women as non-persons as 'the policy of the law ... thought women unfit to judge of public things, [placing] them upon a footing with infants ...'

Shortly before Anthony's trial, thousands of British women registered to vote. In 'British Women's Emancipation', Helena Wojtczak recounts 1,245 women registering in Salford, 1,066 in Aberdeen, 300 in Southwark, 5,750 in Manchester, 559 in Birmingham and 239 in Edinburgh, numbers unknown in Warwickshire, Wales, Kent, East Surrey, North Staffordshire, East Devon and Leeds, because all 'persons' entitled to vote should be registered.[13] Once registered, revising barristers could remove names. Some names survived while most were deleted, thus prompting court

DOI: 10.1057/9781137562357.0004

protest. Along with 5,346 women removed by revising barristers, Mary Abbott took up the challenge, declaring her right to be registered and thus her right to vote in parliamentary elections.

In 1868, *Chorlton v. Lings* addressed three issues: first, women's usage or entitlement to vote before the 1832 Reform Act; secondly, that Act's limitation of extended voting entitlements to 'male persons'; thirdly, the impact of the Representation of the People Act 1867 stating 'every "man" shall be entitled to be registered as a voter ...', in conjunction with Lord Brougham's 1850 Act.

Section 27 of the Reform Act said that in every city or borough returning a member or members of Parliament, every male person of full age who paid taxes and rates for the poor:

> ...not subject to any legal incapacity, who shall occupy [for 12 months], within such city or borough, or within any place sharing in the election for such city or borough, as owner or tenant, any house, warehouse, counting-house, shop, or other building, being, either separately, or jointly with any land within such city, borough, or place occupied therewith by him as owner, or therewith by him as tenant under the same landlord, of the clear yearly value of not less than 10£, shall, if duly registered..., be entitled to vote in the election of... members to serve in any future parliament...

It was important to establish that at least some women met the requirements as the Act preserved voting rights anyone held before the Act became law. Otherwise, in referring explicitly to 'male person', the Reform Act could deprive all women of the right to vote: women's sole right to vote would rely upon the Representation of the People Act. There, courts must be persuaded to interpret 'man' according to the principle that 'unless stated to the contrary' it included woman.

For Bovill, CJ the 'general question' of the desirability of women voting for members of Parliament was irrelevant.[14] Rather, do women 'by law now possess that right' and are women 'included under the words "every man"', or are women 'subject to legal incapacity'? Albeit contending for Abbott that women had a common law right to vote, Coleridge QC (with barrister Dr Richard Pankhurst) had not, Bovill said, produced any instance of women exercising that right. Yet Coleridge had provided instances of 15th- and 16th-century women voting and assisting in legislative deliberations. Bovill acknowledged this, yet accepted no contradiction of his central argument. He contended that such instances were 'of comparatively little weight' against 'the uninterrupted usage to the contrary for several centuries'.

DOI: 10.1057/9781137562357.0004

If a woman appeared to have acted as a returning officer, this was employed to rule out previous instances of women's voting (as with Lady Packington) by the assertion that the voting record was wrong, and the woman must have been a returning officer only. Contrary jurisprudential writings were ignored, whilst those opposing women's right to vote were elevated to authority. Hence, jurists Coke (1552–1634) and Serjeant Heywood (1753–1828) were promoted over jurist Selden (1584–1654). Sadly, despite extending Magna Carta to villeins, Coke was unable to effect this transmutation of meaning for women. Despite 650 years passing since Runnymede, almost 250 after Coke's *Institutes*, once again Magna Carta's 'living' status or 'adaptability' made no mark on women's (lack of) status.

Consistent with later 'person' cases, Bovill and his fellow judges first denied any instances of women voting. When they acknowledged women had voted they denied the impact, and then reasserted that no women 'ever' voted, saying this meant women had no right to do so. Apart from the contradiction, judges failed to acknowledge that instances of women voting would come to a court's attention only if an election result was disputed because, as in *Olive v. Ingram* (1738), a disgruntled loser challenged his successful rival contending women's votes 'tainted' the rival's majority.

As for 'man' including 'woman' in the Representation of the People Act, Bovill said this did not apply. An earlier Act of Parliament could not bind a later Act, and although there is 'no doubt that, in many statutes, "men" may be properly held to include women ... in others it would be ridiculous to suppose the word was used in any other sense than as designating the male sex ...'. To ascertain the legislature's meaning, subject matter and 'general scope and language' of a later Act must be considered, and Bovill 'collected' no intention from the Act's language 'to alter the description of the *persons* who were to vote'. On the contrary, 'the object was, to deal with their *qualification* ...'. If Parliament had intended to extend the vote to women, he concluded, Parliament would have said so explicitly. Besides, women were simply 'incapacitated' from voting.

Albeit he, like Bovill, said there was no need to expound upon the cause of women's incapacity, echoing Blackstone, Willes, J. did just that:

> ... fickleness of judgment and liability to influence have sometimes been suggested ... I must protest against its being supposed to arise in this country from any underrating of the sex either in point of intellect or worth. That would be quite inconsistent with one of the glories of our civilization – the respect and honour in which women are held ...

DOI: 10.1057/9781137562357.0004

That year in Scotland, judges in *Brown v. Ingram* (1868) unanimously denied Mary Brown's right to vote, saying that the sheriff properly struck her name off the roll. Why? Because the Reform Act saved all 'existing laws and customs' relating to voting, and there was 'a long and uninterrupted custom in Scotland limiting the franchise to males'.[15]

Hence, in 1868 more than 8,000 women who registered, and more than 5,000 who protested against their peremptory removal, were expected to consider themselves respected and honoured – merely 'non-persons' disentitled to vote and disregarded when objecting.

Such judicial 'reasoning' continued in *De Souza v. Cobden* [1891]: a woman could be a 'person' for the purpose of criminal action, yet simultaneously be non-personed for adopting the very status whereby she was considered an offender. Miss Cobden was elected to the London County Council. Section 73 of the *Local Government Act 1888* said that a municipal election not disputed within twelve months following election would be deemed to have been to all intents a good and valid election. Twelve months elapsing without challenge, Cobden took her place. Section 41 said any person would be liable to a fine if acting in a corporate office without being qualified. Cobden was prosecuted and found guilty of having voted five times as a member of the Council.

Relying on *Beresford-Hope v. Lady Sandhurst* (1889), the English Court of Appeal upheld the conviction for Coleridge, CJ with a bench of five had said women were 'incapacitated' from being elected members of a county council as they were not qualified 'persons'. The 1,986 votes for Lady Sandhurst were 'thrown away'. Mr Beresford-Hope, albeit losing the election with 1,686 votes, took her place.

Thus, despite accepting that under section 73 her election was beyond question, Cobden was deemed not properly elected, as not being a qualified 'person'. She could be prosecuted, tried and convicted as a 'person acting in a corporate office without being qualified'. Fry, LJ compared Cobden's election to that of a dead man, or 'an inanimate thing which cannot be elected'.[16]

This approach had global appeal. In *Ex parte Ogden* (1893), Foster, J. asked whether, were a Newfoundland dog's name included on the New South Wales electoral roll, 'would he be an elector?' Windeyer, J. believed if someone came forward 'representing himself to be a person whose name is on the roll, but who is dead' the proper response was 'you cannot vote'. Similarly, the proper reply to a married woman was 'you are

DOI: 10.1057/9781137562357.0004

not entitled to vote, in the eye of the law you are non-existent'. Mesdames Lipscombe and White's votes were discounted.[17] But courts did not limit women's non-personhood to voting rights or standing for public office. Women were refused access to education and the professions, too.

In the 1890s, Ada E. Evans enrolled in law at the University of Sydney – fortuitously (or perhaps by design) in the Dean, Professor Pitt-Cobbitt's absence. Upon his return from sabbatical leave, the law school resounded with the bashing and crashing of chairs, desk thumping, and banging of doors. Unhappy that a woman presumed to enter the faculty, much less be accepted into it, Pitt-Cobbitt declared Evans would be better suited to medicine. Nevertheless, Evans stayed, did well and became Sydney's first female law graduate. Obstacles confronted her after graduation, but unlike Sophia Jex-Blake, Evans did not go to court to plead her right to a tertiary education.[18]

Twenty years earlier, the Jex-Blake saga began when she enrolled and successfully completed her first year at Edinburgh University. Correspondence from 1873 indicates at least ten other women were similarly minded: written by Jex-Blake, additional signatories included Edith Pechey, AR Barker, Alice JS Ker, Elizabeth J. Walker, Agnes McLaren, Isa Foggo, Jane R. Robson, Elizabeth Vinson and Jane Massingberd-Mundy. The letter came after the struggle with Edinburgh University had culminated in the House of Lords. There, Jex-Blake, Louisa Stevenson and five others mounted a suit asserting their right to complete medical studies and graduate, their goal, unsurprisingly, to practice medicine. The letter noted:

> The most general objection to the admission of women to Universities lies in the supposed difficulty of educating them jointly with male students of medicine. This may apply to every university in the kingdom except ... St Andrews [having no male medical students].[19]

University regulations said a 'person' with requisite qualifications could be admitted to study. Jex-Blake was admitted. However, some professors objected to teaching women – particularly anatomy and dissection of dead bodies. Male students' objections culminated in a riot. In *Craig v. Jex-Blake* (1871), Jex-Blake was sued for slander, having commented:

> And at last came the day of that disgraceful riot, when the college gates were shut in our face, and our little band bespattered with mud from head to foot. This I do know, that the riot was not wholly or mainly due to men from Surgeons' Hall. I know that Dr Christison's class assistant [Mr Craig] was one

DOI: 10.1057/9781137562357.0004

of the leaders ... , and that the foul language he used could only be explained on the supposition I heard asserted that he was intoxicated ... [20]

Craig was awarded a farthing (half a half-penny) in damages. Under the Senate's new rules, 'women' could study medicine, with 'instruction in separate classes confined entirely to women'. Separate 'women only' classes could be held. *Jex-Blake v. Senatus of University of Edinburgh* (1873) questioned the new regulations' validity, and whether women could be permitted to study as 'women' or 'persons'. Particularly, were women entitled to graduate? Specific requests were, in the alternative, to:

▸ extend to female students the privilege granted by ordinance, namely of qualifying for graduation by their lectures;
▸ authorise appointment of special lecturers providing qualifying courses of instruction in place of professors declining to do so;
▸ ordain that professors be required to give the necessary course of instruction to women.

The Senate Court was divided, with some rebutting the right to make the new rules, effectively denying women any rights vis-à-vis the university (the right to donate funds to it, as women did, was not addressed). While others held that although 'ladies' had through disuse 'lost their claim to be admitted to the University as of right', university authorities could make the rules and, if the women would accept 'certificates of proficiency' (not degrees), 'such arrangements' would be considered.[21] This reflected the 19th-century Oxbridge struggle, where women were denied entry to (men's) colleges and the right to degrees until the following century, albeit Cambridge Girtonians took the tripos, excelling in examinations.[22]

In the House of Lords, not only did the word 'person' play a part, so did 'college' and 'university'. Although (being conferred 'by custom and wont') men's degrees were not to be forfeited, judges denied colleges had rights to confer degrees, saying Edinburgh, a college, had wrongly awarded them.[23] Jex-Blake's counsel observed that 'college' and 'university', used interchangeably, meant the same thing: a chartered institution of higher learning (no doubt just as 'person' meant 'woman' as much as it meant 'man'). Essentially, however, this was a diversion, for if by 'custom and wont' degrees were properly granted, why could women not claim this right? Jex-Blake and her confreres listed women graduating from universities in Germany, Holland, Switzerland, Spain, France and Italy, with women filling professorial chairs at Bologna and Padua.

DOI: 10.1057/9781137562357.0004

Nevertheless, even the most self-professed sympathetic of judges saw womanhood as fatal. Albeit separate classes were impossible in practice, if they wished to study medicine women would, concluded Lord Ardmillan, have to follow this (unviable) path. Few held 'intelligent and virtuous women in higher estimation' than he, and Ardmillan 'fully and respectfully recognise[d] the high qualities, capacities, and vocation of women'.[24] However, women's 'elevation ... in domestic and social position' was Christianity's 'blessed fruit'. So, 'for their own sake' and due to 'the respect' he held for them, his 'duty' lay in his 'decided opinion', namely:

> ... promiscuous attendance of men and women in mixed classes of ... anatomy, surgery, and obstetric science, [and] dissection, demonstration, and clinical exposition, is a thing so unbecoming and so shocking – so perilous to the delicacy and purity of the female sex – to the very crown and charge of womanhood – and so reacting on the spirit and sentiment which sustains the courtesy, reverence, and tenderness of manhood – that the law and constitution of the University, bound to promote, and seeking to promote, the advancement of morality as well as knowledge, cannot sanction or accept such attendance'.

Asking rhetorically how they could attend women-only classes, when no such classes could exist: who would teach them? Could the University sustain them? What power to proclaim them? Lord Ormidale ruled women out of contention altogether. Rules admitting women could not qualify as 'improvement in the University's internal arrangements', so were ultra vires. Anyway, from its inception men had studied there. Omitted from the original regulations, women could not be included now. Lord Benholme agreed. Albeit observing 'knowledge is power', he considered it irrelevant to women who were not entitled to matriculate and be educated at university 'just as if they were males'.

For Lord Neaves, the law recognised sex difference as 'established and well-known', cutting women from various duties, privileges and powers. 'Very weighty reasons [operating] on the national mind' excluded women from universities.[25] Despite women's equally 'noble' 'powers and susceptibilities' they lacked men's 'power of intense labour'. Exposing 'our young females' to the 'severe and incessant work' required for learning would be regrettable. Disregarding women's inequality would destroy 'any scheme of public instruction':

> ... for, as ... the general mass of an army cannot move more rapidly than its weakest and slowest portion, so a general course of study must be toned and

DOI: 10.1057/9781137562357.0004

tempered down to suit the average of all the classes of students for whom it is intended, and that average will always be lowered by the existence of [those unable to] keep pace with the rest.

Women must acquire 'special accomplishments' in household, family and 'ornamental parts of education [tending] so much to social refinement and domestic happiness ...'. Feminine instruction would undermine women's capacity for 'severe pursuits', and university knowledge would not compensate for lack of 'feminine arts and attractions'. The existence of 'remarkable' and 'exceptional' women was immaterial, for 'hasty attachments and premature entanglements' might blight their future lives. Only a 'bold man' would collect women and men together at college, 'whatever number of chaperones he might [bring] to guard them'.

Despite not all judges agreeing, the *Jex-Blake case* ended; although she and most of the others gained medical qualifications elsewhere, entering into practice. Still, Neaves' lament resonated. That same year, Susan B. Anthony, Mary Abbott, Myra Bradwell and Mary Brown – with the thousands of others who registered – were denied their personhood. In *Bradwell v. The State of Illinois* (1872), the US Supreme Court had an easier time than the US District Court adjudging Anthony's lack of capacity, as Bradwell was a married woman.

The Illinois statute enabling entry into legal practice said 'no person' could be an attorney or counsellor-at-law without a licence. Though not in the court file, Bradwell's marital status was crucial. Refusing her application, the Illinois Supreme Court observed that as a married woman she 'would be bound neither by her express contracts nor by those implied contracts which [are created] between attorney and client ...,'[26] Bradwell appealed.

Bradwell's moral character was not questioned. Rather, her right as a citizen in 'any and every profession, occupation or employment in civil life' was. For the US Supreme Court's Bradley, J., Bradwell's sex limited her rights to a livelihood and income through using her qualifications and brain. 'Certainly' no 'historical fact ... ever [established this] as one of the fundamental privileges and immunities of the sex', he said.[27] Civil law, 'as well as nature herself', has ever recognised 'a wide difference in the respective spheres and destinies of man and woman':

> Man is, or should be, woman's protector and defender. The natural and proper timidity and delicacy which belongs to the female sex evidently unfits it for many of the occupations of civil life ...

DOI: 10.1057/9781137562357.0004

Family organisation, said Bradley, 'founded in the divine ordinance as well as the nature of things' sets the domestic sphere as 'properly belonging to [women's] domain and functions'. Presuming to enter legal practice, Bradwell neglected her family and ignored her place. Adopting a 'distinct and independent career' from her husband was 'repugnant'. Ignoring his earlier assertion in the *Slaughter House cases* (1870) of men's right to engage in every field of employment, Bradley said women had no 'fundamental right and privilege' to enter 'every office and position, including those [requiring] highly special qualifications and demanding special responsibilities'. Rather, avenues for 'woman's advancement' and 'occupations adapted to her condition and sex' had his 'heartiest concurrence'. Unmarried women as 'exceptions to the general rule' were not affected by marital 'duties, complications and incapacities', however, 'exceptional cases' should not govern 'civil society's rules'. The 'Creator's law' set women's 'paramount destiny and mission...to fulfil the noble and benign offices of wife and mother'.

The Person Cases – Mark 2

Twenty-five years on, judicial enlightenment remained imperceptible. Neither Magna Carta's 'adaptability' nor 'living nature' featured. Emulating Bradwell, Margaret HS Hall in Scotland and Edyth Haynes in Western Australia took action. In *Margaret HS Hall (for admission to Law Agents Examination)* (1901), Hall was refused admission to the law agent's examination when she and other women applied. The Examiners' Secretary told Hall to present a 'short petition...praying the Court to direct the examiners' to enrol her as a candidate'.[28] When she did, the Law Agents Society said that although women 'practise the profession...in the [US][29] and...by special legislation, women [became] eligible for admission to the Bar in France ...', no woman had been admitted to practice in Scotland, England or Ireland 'at any time'. Thus, 'inveterate usage and custom' confined all departments of law 'exclusively to men'. Nonetheless, the Society finally declared it 'not in their interest or duty to maintain that women ought not to be enrolled as law agents'. However, the First Division Court, consulting nine Law Lords, refused Hall's petition unanimously. Relying on *Brown v. Ingram* (1868), *Jex-Blake* (1873) and *Lady Sandhurst's case* (1889), the Lords' opinion prevailed. Applying equally to male and female that 'persons' was 'ambiguous'. No woman

DOI: 10.1057/9781137562357.0004

had ever been a law agent, thus 'inveterate usage' confined it to male persons. Legislative endorsement, not court action, was required.

More robust than its Scottish counterpart, in 1896 the Western Australian Barristers and Solicitors Admission Board registered Haynes' articles. The Supreme Court refused her right to sit the final examination and she appealed. It was 1904, still, Coke's 1642 extension of justice to villeins, like Holt's 'adaptability' and Beloff's 'always speaking' principle, failed to deliver Magna Carta's justice to women. Besides being unable to spell her given name correctly, despite having to deal with an unmarried woman (unlike *Bradwell* (1872)), Haynes' court had no difficulty ruling her a non-person, too.

In re Edyth (sic) Haynes (1904), McMillan, J. said admission to the bar encompassed eligibility for admission to the bench. Parliament alone must address such an important change. Burnside, J. agreed. Despite 'lady doctors' existence, there could be no 'lady barristers'; from 'almost time immemorial' the profession comprised the male sex only. The legislature must, 'in their wisdom', decide on the 'desirability or otherwise' of amending the Legal Practitioners Act – which said 'any person' with the requisite qualifications should be admitted. Burnside was unprepared 'to start making law'.[30]

In Britain, Miss Bebb tried. Like Haynes, she was a spinster. Unlike the Western Australian Board, the English Law Society refused to register a woman. Bebb sought:

▸ a declaration that under the Solicitors Act 1843 she was a 'person'; and
▸ a writ of mandamus ordering the Board to admit her to examination; or
▸ an injunction restraining them from refusing to admit her.

Her case came before the Court of Appeal in 1913. Ten years earlier, Bertha Cave's application for admission to Grey's Inn of barristers was refused, despite her counsel citing Coke as authority for women (even wives) litigating in land claims. In a mocking commentary, the *Spectator* (1903) considered apposite the 'no woman has ever done it before' argument. Submissions opposing Bebb's application employed *Bertha Cave's Case* (1903). Evidently, that a woman had *tried* for admission previously had no credence. Applying for admission could not dislodge the contention that 'because women have never done it, women are not supposed

DOI: 10.1057/9781137562357.0004

to do it'. Of course this meant that no woman could or would ever be a 'person' for legal practice.

One judge, Cozens-Hardy, MR, relied on Coke's reference to the *Mirror of Justices'* 300-year-old note that a woman was 'not allowed to be an attorney', for by 'disability' no woman 'has ever been an attorney-at-law'. The Solicitors Act 1843 did not renounce this, Cozens-Hardy said, ignoring the *Mirror of Justices'* notorious unreliability.[31] That 'in point of intelligence and education and competency women – and in particular [Miss Bebb]...a distinguished Oxford student – are at least equal to a great many and, probably, far better than many, ... candidates ...' didn't count.[32]

Swinfen Eady, LJ asserted 'no instance of any woman attorney has, I will not say been brought to our knowledge, but, as far as it is known, ever existed'. Nonetheless 'in early days ... a woman was occasionally appointed the attorney or representative of a litigant', Phillimore, LJ said, yet since law became a profession, 'there is no instance of a woman ever being, or it being considered possible that a woman should be, an attorney or a solicitor'. (Cave and Bebb considered it possible, yet as non-persons – a circular argument – no doubt their opinion was irrelevant.) Besides, he added (the *Bradwell* (1872) argument again):

> [M]arried women, not having an absolute liberty to enter into binding contracts, binding themselves personally, would be unfitted either for entering into articles or for contracting with their clients...

As to spinster Bebb:

> [E]very woman can be married at some time..., [causing] a serious inconvenience if, in the middle of her articles, or... conducting a piece of litigation, a woman was suddenly to be disqualified from contracting by reason of her marriage...

Not until 1923 was a woman, Cornelia Sorabji, called to the English Bar, for (unsurprisingly) Bebb had lost her case.[33] So did women wanting to vote as university graduates for parliamentary representation, and women seeking their place in the House of Lords.

Having won entry to St Andrews and Edinburgh Universities in 1892, in 1906 – before the passage of the Sex Disqualification (Removal) Act 1919 – graduates addressed the first challenge. After the Act, Margaret Haig, Viscountess Rhondda, pursued the second. Judicial minds defeated both.

DOI: 10.1057/9781137562357.0004

Graduates voted for a university MP. In *Nairn & Ors* (1906) women graduates sought to do so. Again, the ordinary meaning of 'person' as including 'individuals of both sexes' stood alongside the judge's view that it was 'ambiguous'. At common law, women were legally incapacitated and not persons; Lord Salvesen averred, endorsing Willes, J.'s avowal, that denying women the vote led not from 'any underrating of the sex,...in...intellect or worth' but 'out of respect to women, and a sense of decorum' excusing women from sharing in public affairs. Echoing Blackstone (1765), Salversen said (mordantly) the case 'at least demonstrated that...some members of the sex...do not value their common law privileges'.[34]

Margaret Nairn went to the House of Lords. In *Nairn v. University of St Andrews* (1908), Lords M'Laren, Pearson and Wardwall were unanimous in their decision. 'Person' was ambiguous and common law ruled. 'Though university graduates, not being 'persons', women could not vote; otherwise, a law about university entry and graduation would become one about women's voting rights. Yet it *was* a law about voting rights.

Next, the House of Lords defended its turf. Just as Western Australian Supreme Court judges feared women's ascent to the bench, so did the Lords. *Viscountess Rhondda's Claim* [1922] exercised the minds of twenty-nine Privileges Committee members. Certainly, if anyone ought to win Magna Carta rights, as a peeress in her own right, along with other peeresses represented, Margaret Haig should. But Magna Carta did not feature. The Sex Disqualification (Removal) Act 1919 did. As in *Jex-Blake* (1873), not all agreed that women are not persons, but the majority did.

Without brothers, Haig succeeded to the title upon her father's death. She sought a writ of summons calling her to the Lords. Initially, the Privileges Committee agreed. Days later, Viscount Birkenhead, LC had the matter referred back to the Committee. Haig's case was that immediately before the Act , but for her sex she was entitled to a writ, thence taking her seat in the Lords. Incapacity to receive the writ was a disqualification to exercise a public function. The Act removed that disqualification.

Birkenhead agreed that since the 17th century, constitutional struggle ensured that the Crown could not refuse a new peer a summons to Parliament. Hereditary descent, not royal will, was key. However, Birkenhead concluded that rather than a public office, a peerage conferred a personal right to sit and vote. A (male) minor could attain majority and receive a writ. A woman could not. Applying to public office

DOI: 10.1057/9781137562357.0004

alone, the 1999 Act made no difference. It conferred a right on women to vote in the House of Commons elections, which did not apply to the Lords. Haigh could not have both. Hence, no hereditary entitlement.

Contrarily, Viscount Haldane and Lord Wrenbury resolutely affirmed that Haig could and should take her Lords seat. For Haldane, the only bar against a peeress sitting in the Lords was the common law disqualification, which had ended in 1919 with the Lords' assent to the Act. Haig and others of her status had a right to a writ. Wrenbury agreed that that was a right of a peer, not a 'male peer'. Just as a minor qualifies, disqualification removed by attaining his majority, so for a woman – disqualification of sex being removed by the Act. Wrenbury drubbed the notion that this was a private and not a public office. 'Our Lordships' sitting in a legislative capacity are 'exercising a public function', he said. When sitting judicially:

> [N]o one could dispute that, in reviewing [a Court's] decision... it is exercising the function of reversing, if... so require[d], the decision of a public Court clothed with the power of making orders... binding upon the parties... [35]

Rising at 3.45pm from exercising its judicial function and resuming at 4.15pm for legislative business, 'is it possible to contend ... [the Lords] has ceased to exercise a function, or... its function is not public?' Furthermore, the Act resulted from 'the long and acute struggle of women [for] political and civil equality with men... asserting [as] their due... complete equality of men and women' in the House of Lords and anywhere else. 'Reading it from one end to the other', nothing confined or curtailed the 'perfect generality' of 'any public function'. Asserting 'this particular function is so important... it cannot be affected except by express words' is impossible, unless, 'upon true principle of construction', something excludes it from the general words, then 'it is included in them, however important it may be ...'

Haldane and Wrenbury lost. So did Haig. Yet England's Privy Council heralded change. Beloff's characterisation of Magna Carta as an 'always speaking statute' applied to the British North America Act, winning women personhood.

'Does the word "persons" in section 24 of the British North America Act 1867 include female persons?' Dubbed 'the Famous Five', Canadians Henrietta Muir Edwards, Nellie L. McClung, Louise C. McKinney, Emily F. Murphy and Irene Parlby, said it did. In *Edwards v. AG of Canada* [1928], five Canadian Supreme Court judges disagreed. In *Edwards v. AG*

DOI: 10.1057/9781137562357.0004

of Canada [1929], five privy councillors overturned them, holding unanimously that, being persons, women could become Canadian senators. The judgment's initial words, 'The exclusion of women from all public offices is a relic of days more barbarous than ours ...', presaged the outcome. History, like Magna Carta, does not remain static. It was no argument that no woman 'had served or ... claimed to serve' in public office, for then the point could never be contested and no claim could ever be made.

> Customs are apt to develop into traditions which are stronger than law and remain unchallenged long after the reason for them has disappeared.[36]

Hence, any 'appeal to history' as to 'ambiguity' in the word 'person' is 'not conclusive'. Reasonings 'commending themselves ... to those ... apply[ing] the law in different circumstances, in different centuries to countries in different stages of development', could not 'apply rigidly' to decisions for contemporary Canada. The 1867 Act was a constitution for a 'new country'.

Were women eligible to be senators in Canada's upper house? Neither male nor female had a right of summons. Did the governor-general have a right to summon women (with men)? The Act's first section referring to 'person' said the governor-general would choose and summon 'persons' who are members of the Privy Council'. Here, 'person' included members of both sexes. The Senate was to consist of 72 'members', a word 'not in ordinary English confined to male persons'. For those asking why 'person' should include females, 'the obvious answer is why should it not?' Those disagreeing 'must make out their case'.

The governor-general summoned 'qualified persons'. 'Persons' including male and female, but what did 'qualified' mean? The Act's qualifications included being a natural born subject naturalised by the law of Great Britain, any provincial legislature before the union of Canada, or the Canadian Parliament after union. Married women under the Aliens Act 1844 did not take their husband's nationality, being deemed naturalised in their own right. If there were any property qualification, women were not excluded as Married Women's Property Acts said married women could hold property in their own right. Other sections used 'person' to include women and men, one saying court pleadings could be in English or French: '... it can hardly have been supposed that a man might use either the English or the French language but a woman might not ...'

Finally, the Privy Council referenced John Stuart Mill's proposed 1867 Representation of the People Bill amendment to omit 'man' and substitute it with 'person'. Mill's vision of women as persons triumphed. In 1930s Canada, women (being persons) were entitled to be called to the Senate. Like Beloff's 'always speaking' Magna Carta, the British North America Act is 'a living tree capable of growth and expansion within its natural limits'. So seemingly ended several hundred years of women being deemed non-persons – as courts wished.

When is a person not one?

When deemed non-persons, women could accept it, go to the legislature, or continue legal challenges. Ada E. Evans took both paths. As a non-person she was denied the right to register as a student-at-law, then denied the right to practice as a barrister. Graduating in law in 1902, she lobbied successive attorneys-general until the passage of the Women's Legal Status Act 1918, giving her the right to be registered as a student-at-law. In 1921 she was admitted to the NSW Bar. By then, despite her redoubtable capacities she doubted her ability to practice – so encouraged others to take up the challenge.[37]

Yet as *Re Kitson* [1920] illustrates, the legislative path solved one problem while creating another. In 1911, the Female Law Practitioners Act affirmed *women's* entitlement to legal practice. In 1920, lawyer Mary Cecil Kitson was refused admission as a notary public, because the Public Notaries Act 1859 (SA) referred to 'every person' satisfying the court of 'fitness and qualifications'. Because 'woman' was not in that Act, Kitson was refused, despite being qualified to perform the duties and exercise the functions of the office. She qualified under that Act , and under Magna Carta's cap. 45 which required knowledge of the law for such offices.[38] By winning on the one hand – legislative imprimatur to practice law – women lost on the other – courts using 'woman' Acts to affirm that 'person' appearing in other Acts was not a woman.

Today, women's personhood remains problematic.

In 1989 the Melbourne *Age* reported a Supreme Court appeal against a 'pregnant tribunal's planning decision'. Angela Smith, pregnant at the time, presided. Solicitor Gary Bigmore challenged the decision for errors of law and lack of natural justice in denying a fair hearing. Smith, it was claimed, 'suffered from the well-known medical condition

DOI: 10.1057/9781137562357.0004

(placidity)... detract[ing] significantly from the intellectual competence of all mothers-to-be'. Although Bigmore withdrew the appeal, it indicates a continuing conviction that women are not 'persons' but 'other'.[39]

Personhood is deemed a field of rationality to which men alone belong: biological capacities debar women. Abortion and surrogacy highlight this. Women's lack of personhood is at the core of arguments oppositional to abortion. It underlies surrogacy. The *Baby 'M' Case* (1988), the first where a court grappled with surrogacy, provides a graphic illustration. There, Mary Beth Whitehead gave birth to Sara (Baby 'M') under a contract initially held valid then struck down, whereby the child (using Bill Stern's semen and Whitehead's ovum) went to Stern and his wife. In the first instance, contradictorily the judge said the best interests of the child was determinative, despite the contract's terms categorically stating the child was to go to Stern. The appellate court pinpointed this contradiction, nevertheless holding that the child must go to Stern 'in Baby "M"'s best interests'. Whitehead's having borne the child was irrelevant. She was even denied the right to name the child, Sara becoming 'Melissa'.

That, in the circumstances, Whitehead exercised agency before or at conception is suspect. In any event, she was denied the right to exercise agency after the child's birth. The court considered 'best interests' in favour of the child, not the woman giving birth. The focus is on the child to the exclusion of the mother. A court considering the mother's 'best interests' compromises its decision-making. A 'child's best interests' decision may be consistent with a mother's best interests, but legally this must be coincidental only. In Whitehead's case, she became a receptacle, her interests subjugated by having entered into a contract with a sperm donor. In the end, his status trumped hers for 'best interests' meant that the child was adjudged as better off not with her mother, but with a couple having better financial capacity and standing. Ultimately, financial capacity and standing were directly related to Stern's gender and the advantages of being male – and consistent with *his* 'best interests'.

Notions of 'agency' evaporate when parties to 'agreements' are revealed. In 'A War on Women', Lopez and Sloan report US surrogacy organisations locating near-army bases, a market providing women who for financial reasons are targets. Tertiary students needing financial assistance are targeted too. In 2013, student borrowers carried an average total debt of $30,000. Ten years ago, US student debt was $300 billion; today it is $1.1 trillion. Brent W. Ambrose, Larry Cordell and Shuwei

DOI: 10.1057/9781137562357.0004

Ma's 2015 Federal Reserve Study *The Impact of Student Loan Debt* shows distinctive changes to the US national economy as a consequence. No wonder students are vulnerable.[40]

Also targeted are women with few financial opportunities – from India and Thailand. US capitalist culture might privilege contractual or property rights of 'buyers', but using women for child production is global. International trafficking in babies born of 'poor' women in 'poor' countries infects Australia, Aotearoa/New Zealand, Canada and the UK. Rising by 255% between 2008 and 2014, women from India, Georgia, the Ukraine and US as 'surrogates' have borne children now registered in Britain.[41] In Canada, a website advertises surrogacy contracts costing up to $CAN60,000–76,500 without indicating the 'surrogates' source, and for 'an American donor' up to $CAN176,500. Commercial surrogacy being illegal, in 2011 Aotearoa/New Zealanders were reported as paying 'up to $NZ100,000' for overseas 'surrogates'.[42] All Australian jurisdictions make commercial surrogacy illegal, yet as of June 2013, the Family Court entertained sixteen applications for parental rights of children born commercially in the US (two cases), South Africa (one), Thailand (eight) and India (five). Mary Keyes and Richard Chisholm (2013) in *Commercial Surrogacy* report that between 2008 and 2010 the practice increased by 1000%, '... poor women [being] found who, for a payment, will donate eggs, carry and give birth to a child, then relinquish the child forever to the Australian commissioning couple'.[43] These substantial money sums go principally to commercial providers, not the women, with 'consent' suspect: in *Mason & Mason and Anor* [2013], the judge 'found troubling' the 29-page English language contract bearing the thumbprint of the Indian 'surrogate', she being illiterate in English and Hindi. Still, the child's interests necessarily remain paramount, for they are determined against a fait accompli: children removed from their country of birth (and mother) risk statelessness if the commissioning 'parents' nationality is not conferred.

When women are treated as receptacles, not persons – their capacity for nurturing a foetus and giving birth the criteria upon which they are chosen, along with their financially needy status and vulnerability – it is disingenuous to speak of agency or personhood. In February 2015, Thailand legislated against commercial surrogacy by foreigners, aiming to prevent Thailand from being "the womb of the world".[44]

Regarding abortion, the Abortion Act 1967 (UK)[45] says a pregnancy termination is not illegal if conducted by a registered medical practitioner, two doctors holding the opinion that it was 'formed in good faith' and that the pregnancy is twenty-four weeks or less, and:

‣ its continuation would 'involve risk, greater than if the pregnancy were terminated' of physical or mental health risk to the woman or her children; or
‣ it is necessary to prevent 'grave permanent injury' to the woman's physical or mental health; or
‣ its continuance 'would involve risk to [her] life greater than if the pregnancy were not terminated'; or
‣ there is a substantial risk to the putative child of physical or mental abnormalities so as to be seriously handicapped on birth.

Albeit welcomed as a huge step forward for women, the law undercuts women's autonomy. No other medical operation requires legal authorisation by two practitioners or special dispensation from this requirement. Still, at least women have an acknowledged right, however circumscribed.

Elsewhere, attacks on a woman's right to control her body remain. In Northern Ireland, that the woman is at risk of 'permanent or serious damage' to her mental or physical health without termination is the criterion. Efforts to limit abortions to NHS hospitals, removing women's right to attend a clinic, continue. In 2015 the Justice Department of Ireland proposed excluding rape and incest victims/survivors from abortion law.[46] Meanwhile, in 2012 the Republic of Ireland saw Savita Halapanavar die from septicaemia in a Galway hospital after being refused a termination. Identifying 'a foetal heartbeat', the staff told Halapanavar that Ireland was 'a Catholic country', thus denying her termination request. Religion (and chauvinism) trumped healthcare.[47] The resulting furore generated the Protection of Life in Pregnancy Act 2013. Allowing doctors to terminate upon 'risk of life from physical illness' and 'risk of loss of life from physical illness in emergency', women's healthcare remains bound to religion, not healthcare for women as persons. As Kitty Holland writes in *Savita*, women bearing a foetus from rape or sexual exploitation or diagnosed with an abnormality will continue to travel to England[48] – where the Abortion Act denies autonomy in any event.

US abortion rights under *Roe v. Wade* (1973) suffer constant attack. US promote limiting legislation, Congress bans federal funding, and Planned Parenthood is vilified. Republican politicians condemn women's right to

DOI: 10.1057/9781137562357.0004

abortion. Emphasising women's lack of personhood, arguments elevate dogma over women's right to health care. Religion dictates healthcare access, denying women the right, or capacity, to make decisions about their own bodies. As with surrogacy, in these legislative moves, 'personhood' of a foetus defeats women's entitlement to autonomy and personhood.

Nevertheless, some courts recognise that personhood and abortion are linked. In *R. v. Morgentaler* [1988], Canada's Supreme Court by majority, applying the Canadian Charter of Rights, struck down Criminal Code prohibitions on abortion without a certificate from a therapeutic abortion committee of an accredited or approved hospital. Dickson, CJ and Lamer, J. held state interference 'with bodily integrity' and 'serious state imposed psychological stress...constitutes a breach of security of the person':

> Forcing a woman, by threat of criminal sanction, to carry a foetus to term unless she meets certain criteria unrelated to her own priorities and aspirations, is a profound interference with a woman's body and thus an infringement of security of the person.[49]

The Canadian Supreme Court further confirmed women's personhood in *Trembloy v. Dailgle* [1989] refusing to uphold a restraining order where Chantal Daigle's ex-boyfriend sought to deny her right to abortion anywhere in Canada.

That a woman's decision is determinative has traction in Australia. Although South Australia's law mirrors the UK, Western Australia and Victoria have decriminalised abortion, and New South Wales in *R. v. Wald* (1971) and Queensland in *R. v. Bayliss* (1986), consistent with *R. v. Davidson* [1969], legalise abortion where the life or physical or mental health of the mother is in danger, including risk of foetal damage or potential disability. *CES and Another v. Superclincs* (1995) affirmed this includes economic, social or medical grounds or reasons. In the 1980s, some Australian politicians sought to deny termination payments through Medicare, and some echo US anti-abortion politicians. However, in *R. v. Leach and Brennan* [2010] a Queensland jury acquitted a woman and her partner, charged under the Criminal Code for terminating a pregnancy using the drugs mifepristone and misoprostol obtained privately from overseas, and in *Application of Kathleen May Harrigan* (1982) the High Court demonstrated an aversion to politicisation of abortion law.[50]

DOI: 10.1057/9781137562357.0004

Ultimately, however, that Canada has acknowledged abortion rights as fundamental to women's bodily integrity may be unsurprising. Perhaps Canada's effective translation of the 'freemen' of Magna Carta into 'freewomen' follows logically from that landmark Privy Council decision that the five women plaintiffs, and hence all Canadian women, were persons. Almost 800 years after Magna Carta, sixty years after *Edwards v. AG of Canada* [1929], that decision stands as a template for women's rights. 'Women as persons' has begun to illuminate women's rights.

Notes

1   Beloff, 'Magna Carta', 2015, p. 6; Holt, *Magna Carta*, 2015, pp. 40, 41.
2   Pizan, *The Treasure*, 1405, p. 142.
3   Lawson, 'Introduction', in Pizan, *The Treasure*, 1985, 2008, p. xviii.
4   *Commentaries*, vol. 1, 1765, pp. 442–445.
5   Pizan, *The Treasure*, 1405, p. 121.
6   Leyser, *Medieval Women*, 1995, p. 155; citing Tanner, *The Church in Late Medieval Norwich*, 1984.
7   Scutt, *Singular Women*, 1994.
8   Wollstonecraft, *A Vindication*, 1792, 2004, p. 96.
9   *Commentaries*, 1765, 1793 edn, vol. 1, p. 445, fn.
10 Holt, *Magna Carta*, 2015, pp. 39–40.
11 Linder, 'Trial of Susan B. Anthony', 2001; following quotations from Linder, p. 9.
12 *Olive v. Ingram* (1738); following quotations from that case, at 263–268, 269, 271, 273.
13 Wojtczak, *British Women's Emancipation*, 2009.
14 *Chorlton v. Lings* (1868–1869), at 383; following quotations from that case, at 382, 383, 384–387 (Bovill), 376, 377, 388, 389–392 (Willes), 392–394 (Byles), 394–397 (Keating).
15 *Brown v. Ingram* (1868), at 281.
16 *De Souza v. Cobden* [1891], at 692.
17 *Ex parte Ogden* (1893), at 88.
18 Scutt, *Women and the Law*, 1990.
19 Lis Smith unearthed the letter: University of St Andrews, 'Dr No', 2012; Smith, 'A Woman is a Person!' 2012.
20 *Craig v. Jex-Blake* (1871), at 974.
21 *Jex-Blake* (1873), at 786–787.

22 Oxford women gained degrees in 1920; Cambridge 1948: Herstoria, *Women's Access*, 2012.

23 *Jex-Blake* (1873), at 811.

24 *Jex-Blake* (1873), at 833–834.

25 *In re Bradwell* 55 Ill. 535 (1869), at 537; cited *Bradwell v. The State* (1872), at 131.

26 *Bradwell v. The State* (1872), at 141; following quotations from that case, at 142.

27 *Nairn & Ors* (1906), 179.

28 *Margaret HS Hall* (1901), at 1060; following quotations from that case, at 1063, 1065.

29 Weisberg, 'Barred from the Bar', 1977.

30 *In re Edith Hanes* (1904), at 213–214 (Burnside), 213 (McMillan).

31 See Frankfurter, 'The Supreme Court', 1957.

32 *Bebb v. Law Society* (1913)[1914], at 294 (Cozens-Hardy), 295 (Swifen Eady), 297–298, 299 (Phillimore).

33 On Sorabji, see Midgley, 'Ethnicity, "race" and empire', 1995, p. 260.

34 *Nairn & Ors* (1906), at 179.

35 Viscountess Rhondda's Claim [1922], at 374, 381.

36 *Edwards v. AG of Canada* [1929], at 2; following quotations that case 128, 135, 138, 143.

37 Scutt, *Women and the Law*, 1990; 'The Glory of a Pioneer', Ada Evans Chambers, Sydney.

38 *Re Kitson* [1920], at 231.

39 Scutt, *Women and the Law*, 1990, pp. 563–564.

40 news.com.au, 'Babies – ', 2014; Kirby, 'These two', 2013.

41 Dugan, 'Revealed: Surrogate births', 2015.

42 Surrogacy in Canada OnLine, 'Cost of surrogacy'; BBC News, 'Thailand bans', 2015; Dugan, 'Revealed: Surrogate births', 2015; Dastheib, 'Rent-a-womb'.

43 Keyes and Chisholm, *Commercial Surrgacy*, 2013, p. 1, 3.

44 BBC News, 'Thailand bans', 2015; Dastheib, 'Rent-a-womb'.

45 Unproclaimed in NI. For UK generally Welstead and Edwards, *Family Law*, 2013, pp. 324–333.

46 BBC, 'Abortion law', 2015; McDonald, 'Northern Ireland', 2015.

47 BBC, 'Woman dies', 2012.

48 Holland, *Savita*, 2013, p. 158.

49 *R. v. Morgantaler* [1988], at 32, 39; Pro-Choice Action Network, 1999.

50 Scutt, *Women and the Law*, 1990, pp. 173–187.

DOI: 10.1057/9781137562357.0004

3

Are Women Peers?

Abstract: *Under Magna Carta, freemen were judged by peers. As Scutt observes, women tried, convicted and hanged by all-male juries and judges, prosecuted by men and represented by male defence counsel lacked jury rights. Women were condemned as witches because Hale said witches existed in law and the Bible. As 'non-persons', women could not be jurors, judges, prosecutors or defence counsel. Susan B. Anthony and Elizabeth Cady Stanton asserted women's jury rights. Canadian, US, UK, Aotearoa/ New Zealand and Australian women campaigned for jury rights equal to men. Defence counsel said women favoured accused in rape cases, then claimed women favoured rape victims/survivors. Only in the late 20th century were women acknowledged as 'peers', to sit, like men, on juries deciding guilt or innocence – of women and men alike.*

Keywords: Jury Acts; women and courts; women and juries; women as accused; women as defendants; women as jurors; women's jury campaigns

Scutt, Jocelynne A. *Women and Magna Carta: A Treaty for Rights or Wrongs?* Basingstoke: Palgrave Macmillan, 2016. DOI: 10.1057/9781137562357.0005.

> No freeman shall be arrested or imprisoned or disseised or outlawed
> or exiled or in any way victimised ... except by the lawful judgment
> of his peers ...
>
> *Magna Carta, cap. 39*

Guilty of artifice, guilty as charged?

On 9 January 1923, convicted of murdering her husband, Edith Thompson
was hanged at London's Holloway Prison. Frederick Bywaters struck
the knife blows killing Percy Thompson. Bywaters and Thompson were
charged with murder in concert. The jury, comprising eleven men and
one woman, deliberated for just over two hours and despite Bywaters'
continuing protestations denying Thompson's involvement, both were
found guilty.

At the Old Bailey and London Sessions two years before, for the first
time women were called for jury service. Although Magna Carta spoke
of lawful judgment by peers, Holt observes that the principle was 'open
to interpretation', as women were not 'persons' in the UK nor were they,
until 1921, 'peers'.[1] Thomson had one of her peers sit in judgment. It did
not save her. She and that lone juror were the only women in the trial.
For Thomson, the judge was male, the prosecutor male, the defence team
male, and tipstaff male.

A legal system with an irrefutably masculine face confronted women
under British justice. Precluded from voting, standing for Parliament or
being selected for winnable seats, no woman could be tried under laws
made by women. Denied the right to attend university or enter articles-
of-clerkship, no women could qualify for admission to legal practice,
none could take a client's instructions or represent any woman at the bar.
Once qualified and called, women rarely if ever worked as juniors with
KCs or QCs and so lacked jury trial expertise. While women, however
learned and skilled, were regarded as 'unqualified' for judicial appointment, or simply not considered at all, no woman could be tried before a
female judge.

Bywaters was convicted because he stabbed a man to death. Thompson
was convicted because, as a married woman, she had committed adultery
and written mad, passionate letters to Bywaters, her lover. In his *Trial of
Frederick Bywaters*, Filson Young identifies courtroom theatre involving

DOI: 10.1057/9781137562357.0005

passionate ardour and criminal lawyers with 'an incorrigible instinct for melodrama ... apt to see, or rather present, everyone in the light of martyr, hero, or villain'.[2] Some might 'scorn to ... divide' human nature into 'two kinds of people', yet courts are presented with, on one side:

> ... plain, decent people, the stuff of which judges and juries are made, ... shocked and horrified at any transgression of the moral law, ... hardly believ[ing] persons should be found wicked enough to transgress it; on the other ..., blackguards and devils, degraded by such things as passion; guilty, outside licensed degrees, of a thing called love; and generally and deservedly in trouble of some kind until ... swept within the meshes of the law.

Young concludes the Bywaters-Thompson case was no different:

> The three persons concerned were duly presented in the melodramatic way. The good, patient and unoffending husband; the manly young fellow, corrupted and debauched by the experienced woman of the world; and the black-hearted sorceress, weaving her skills, casting her nets, ... bringing ruin on everyone connected with her.

Through fictional character Julia Starling, in *A Pin to See the Peepshow*, F. Tennyson Jesse paints a picture of Thompson at her trial. Julia winsome. Julia attractive. Julia with a smile she believes will melt the hearts and sway the minds of judge and jury. Julia with a 'good' side, revealed when she tilts her head 'just so'. Yet none of it, the artifice, the true innocence, the fantasy that so long as she wears dainty gloves, delicate seersucker, voile or flora cotton (no large print blossoms, of course), discreet and tasteful linen draped artfully across discreet and gently curving bosom, 'forgetting' to wear her glasses, so 'they' will simply know she's not guilty, none of it works. Still, into the jury's care she commends herself, giving evidence despite counsel's warning not to:

> She had always been able to make men believe what she said. Why should this be different, especially when she knew she was telling the truth?[3]

In *What Are You? A Woman I Suppose,* Jessica A. Gibson describes women filling a variety of roles at the 18th-century Old Bailey. Contrary to conventional history,[4] women appeared not only as defendants, but as principal witnesses in robbery, rape and theft, and as witnesses in those crimes as well as manslaughter and murder.

In 1786, the year Gibson researched, 40% of women at the Old Bailey were witnesses and 36% defendants. The first two assize court sessions that year saw 817 men and 156 women in 202 cases, thirty-two women

DOI: 10.1057/9781137562357.0005

defendants, thirty-nine principal witnesses ('prosecutrixes') and eighty-four witnesses including character witnesses. One appeared in absentia, her death at the trial's heart.[5]

Mirroring how judges and juries (all male) might relate to them, women adopted various positions, consistent with their genuine differences. Some defendants claimed disadvantage and despair, hardship and distress. Some were assertive, defiant and bold. Determining whether these approaches were genuine or contrived is difficult. However, the women knew their future was dependent solely upon the way men in authority in the courtroom saw and assessed them. Living in a male-dominated world influenced their everyday lives. The law's majesty and unfamiliarity of the courtroom made male authority even more absolute. Still, some women were conversant with courtrooms through attending trials. They saw other women on trial or as witnesses, gauging the impact of women's approaches in giving evidence or seeking absolution through a plea for mercy.

When Thompson became the 'delicate damsel', she followed a tradition criminologists claim instigates more lenient treatment of female defendants. However, the claim ignores women's lesser criminal histories and types of offence for which women are prosecuted, and so is easily challenged. Indeed, women may be more harshly treated. Any 18th-century woman who believed claiming 'great difficulty or weakness [meant she] would receive the court's mercy' learned this was an uncertain strategy (if strategy it was).

Gibson found that women asserting a defence of distress or hardship met with mixed results. Accused of stealing linen, citing her husband's illness, Hanna Hooper maintained she was 'starving to death'. After being 'passed to [her] parish', she left, fretting and distressed, abandoning her children. Her landlady 'knew of [her] distresses', Hooper added, saying she'd come 'sixty miles from home' to fetch her family, her husband leaving her 'a stranger in town [where she] pawned all [her] clothes and ... sheets to support [her] family'.

Hooper and three more claiming ill or dying children or sick or distressed husbands were found guilty. Three others pleaded similarly and, though found guilty, gained recommendations for mercy. For one, an explanation similar to Hoopers' followed the prosecution's plea for pity – a deceased husband, recent birth of a child, uncertainty about her husband's parish, and absence of friends or support. Outcomes differed: Hooper summarily convicted, this woman's pleas granted mercy.

DOI: 10.1057/9781137562357.0005

Women were asked their marital status. Pleading marital coercion if her husband was present meant a married woman escaped conviction. However, this was not the sole or compelling reason for asking. Gibson's research shows the query arising even in trials for murder, which (with treason) marital coercion did not excuse. Rather than exculpation, the question more often went to condemnation: disclosing women 'living in sin', working as prostitutes, or engaged in serial relationships – all going to character. As Gibson says, 'wives were held to higher moral standards than their husbands'. If single, with no man to control her, a female was a 'loose woman', attracting the court's condemnation.

Men's marital status was not asked, not because they could not plead marital coercion, but because marital status did not define them. Men pleaded hardship, distress and household responsibilities which might be accepted or dismissed, too. Yet they appeared before male judges and juries. Though often facing class distinctions, the stark difference confronting women disappeared. Not only was gender difference absent. Whether defendants, principal witnesses or witnesses, consistent with Magna Carta, men appeared in a system built by men. Women's appearance in roles other than defendant, even as matron-jurors in pregnancy pleas, gave them no power to determine the structure or construction of justice. Whatever women's input, courts were in the ultimate sense and reality, men's domain.

A jury of her peers

On 12 January 1921, the *Manchester Guardian* reported on women for the first time serving on juries in London Central Criminal Court. Ten men and two women heard a plea of 'guilty' to bigamy. The deceived woman told the court that throughout a lengthy acquaintanceship, the man presented himself as single 'but had always treated her kindly, she respected him, and hoped he would be dealt with leniently'. The journalist – billed as 'A Woman Correspondent'– considered the case of great interest to the women jurors. Meanwhile, Mrs Taylor Bumpstead, the only woman selected in the Court of the Common Serjeant, was chosen as foreman (sic) for this case. At London Sessions, one woman juror sat somewhat unwillingly, but expected women on juries would benefit women:

> Some cases would be very unpleasant, but men had not shirked their duties and women must equally show a public spirit.[6]

DOI: 10.1057/9781137562357.0005

This reversed arguments denying women the right of jury duty. In 1405, Pizan similarly argued in *The Book of the City of Ladies*, first asserting women have no place in the law, women and men's spheres being different, each sex endowed with 'qualities and attributes ... [needed] to perform the tasks for which they are cut out'. Then she acknowledges: 'sometimes humankind fails to respect these distinctions', thus demolishing the initial argument with examples of women acting with distinction in 'men's sphere', including law.[7]

Despite Pizan, ability was not the principle for selecting jurors, judges, prosecutors or counsel. Key was 'is the candidate male?' In mediaeval Britain, women could raise a 'hue and cry' – calling out felons and suspects, urging everyone to the chase, joining in and being witnesses against defendants, as Gibson showed for 18th-century courts. However, women did not, as Helen Cam notes in *The Hundred and the Hundred Rolls*, swear the tithing oath, committing to be 'a lawful man' bearing loyalty to the king and his heirs, and to 'my lord and his heirs', and being 'justiciable to my chief tithing man'.[8] Nevertheless, women could be accused, arrested, tried, convicted and hanged or worse, not escape imprisonment or cruelty by notions of frailty. Women were particularly susceptible to torture, threatened or applied. Cam reports a sheriff's clerk threatening rape and forcible removal of teeth of one woman, thereby intimidating her into hiding.

Without bail, like men, women could be held in the cells, whether a pit or wooden cage, awaiting assizes and judges' attendance. A jury would be selected consisting of twelve men 'and true', the trial ending with a fine, formal sentence of imprisonment, hanging or freedom. An accused might spend months in prison until the hearing, women receiving 'no special treatment or protection'. Cam cites a woman accused of stealing her lady's jewelry taken to Guildford Gaol and languishing forty-seven weeks 'with all the other thieves of the county' before being found 'not guilty' by the all-male jury, and set free.

Though lacking law-making power, women laboured under criminal laws. Men alone could commit rape, women the targets, yet some crimes targeted female offenders only. Women alone were scolds, sentenced to the pillories or ducking stool. In Britain, generally women were those accused, tried and convicted of witchcraft.[9] Magna Carta made no difference. In *Magna Carta* David Carpenter suggests women were protected by some of its provisions, yet his foundation seems unlikely. He surmises that Matilda de Brionze and her eldest son starving to death at John's

DOI: 10.1057/9781137562357.0005

hands in 1210 lay behind Magna Carta's 'insistence that no free man be "destroyed" save by the lawful judgment of his peers or by the law of the land'. Yet founding this provision in Matilda's death is contradicted by the word 'freeman' – inapplicable to any woman. That chapter's ban on outlawry except in the case of 'judgment or law' is applicable, as Carpenter notes, to men alone. Women were 'waived' (made waifs by abandonment) not outlawed. Yet both waifs and outlaws suffered banishment.[10]

Sometimes in Europe, men were equally (France) or more so (Iceland) at risk. However, when criminal laws sanctioned hanging of witches in England and burning at the stake in Scotland, women were persecuted, dying in hundreds, while men charged and convicted were relatively few.[11] This differential persisted in the US too, without any amelioration through Magna Carta.

An obsession with 'Witchcrafte, Inchantment, Charme or Sorcerie, and dealings with evil and wicked Spirits' permeated 16th-century society, the Witchcraft Act 1542 making witchcraft a crime punishable by death. Though repealed in 1547, the Act's 1562 successor was followed by a rise in accusations, trials and convictions. Women in England's south east, the Fens, Bedfordshire, Huntingdonshire and Essex, were particularly at risk. In James I's reign, witch trials peaked under the 1562 Act, which, like its 1604 replacement, transferred witch trials from ecclesiastical to secular courts. With Magna Carta not protecting his targets, Matthew Hale, sometime England's chief justice, came into his own. Not only women of his time were to suffer, but his pronouncements held sway in courts long after his death, their resonance chiming with misogyny.

Can a judge believing in witches be taken seriously as an authority? Amongst almost universal jurisprudential acclaim, William Holdsworth, Vinerian Professor of English Law, thought so.[12]

The first and last recorded English witch trials occurred at Bury St Edmunds. Self-styled witchfinder General Matthew Hopkins led the first and Hale judged the last. Jone Jordan and Joane Nayler (sometimes Naylor) were tried in 1599. Amy Duny (sometimes Denny or Deny) and Rose Cullender were found guilty on 17 March 1682. Between these dates, Wallace Notestein in *A History of Witchcraft* lists, amongst many others, eighteen 'witches' hanged together at Bury St Edmunds on 27 August 1645: Anne Alderman, Rebecca Morris and Mary Bacon of Chattisham; Mary Clowes of Yoxford; Sara Spindler, Jane Linstead, Thomas Everard and Mary Everard of Halesworth; Mary Fuller of

DOI: 10.1057/9781137562357.0005

Combs, near Stowmarket; Jon Lowes of Brandeston; Susan Manners, Jane Rivet and Mary Skipper of Copdock, near Ipswich; Mary Smith of Great Glemham; Margery Sparham of Mendham; Katherine Tooly of Westleton; and Anne Leech and Anne Wright, residence unknown. The cooper and vicar alone were men. The women bore no identity other than their names, except Mary Everard, described as wife of Thomas. All were hanged at Hopkins' instigation.[13]

For Hale, no witchfinder general was required. First published in 1736, *Hale's Pleas of the Crown* was reprinted through the centuries. Duny and Cullender's crimes were listed as bewitching young children exhibiting symptoms including coughing up pins and nails, sometimes thirty simultaneously and some as large as horseshoe nails. Hale advised the jury two matters alone merited enquiry: 'First, whether or no these children were bewitched? Secondly, whether the prisoners at the bar were guilty of it?' He doubted not there were witches, for, first, 'the scriptures affirmed so much' and, secondly, 'the wisdom of all nations had provided laws against such persons, which is an argument of their confidence of such a crime'. Furthermore, that was:

> [T]he judgment of this Kingdom, as appears by that Act of Parliament which hath provided punishments proportionable to the quality of the offence.[14]

The argument's circularity missed Hale's attention: men made laws asserting witches' existence, therefore, witches must exist; men executing those laws, taking witches into custody and bringing them before men finding them guilty and sentencing them, meant witches must exist. That once found guilty they were hanged for the crime in turn affirmed witches' existence: otherwise there could be conviction, no sentence, no execution.

Reverence for Hale continued well into the 20th century. Despite repeal of the Witchcraft Acts *Hale's Pleas* still retains some grip, meaning successive judges, lawyers and traditional legal scholars have avoided his opinions on witchcraft and role in witchcraft trials. If avoidance proves impossible, their justification is as 'of its time'. Holdsworth, Oxford professor and author of *A History of English Law* – seventeen volumes published from 1903 to 1966 – contends the Duny-Cullender hanging 'accord[ed] with the law' for witches' existence 'was vouched for by the *Bible*', therefore '... a man of Hale's mind and temper could hardly be expected to doubt'. In any event, 'these are, after all, small matters'.[15]

DOI: 10.1057/9781137562357.0005

Threatened, terrified, terrorised, tortured – were they able to express it, dead women would have a different view.

Getting on juries – no small matter

In the US, Magna Carta merited high esteem federally. As Susan B. Anthony observed in 1876, with trial by a jury of peers being 'so jealously guarded', states 'refused to ratify the original constitution until ... the 6th Amendment [guaranteed it]'. Despite this, women were denied a jury of peers, meaning 'young girls' were tried, convicted and hanged 'for the crime of infanticide ... while no woman's voice could be heard in their defense'. Twenty years before, speaking in 1854 to the New York legislature, Elizabeth Cady Stanton demand enfranchisement and jury duty rights.[16]

In the UK, (non)person case judges consistently proclaimed women had never sat, and should never sit, on juries. Echoing others, in the *Jex-Blake Case* (1873), Lord Neaves used history to exclude women, combining the 'never sat' mantra with their being 'neither compelled nor qualified' to sit. Yet this categorical statement is undercut by his similarly confident assertion that women's exclusion from being witnesses had a long history, although 'recent legislation' made them competent as instrumentary witnesses. The dissonance between what judges in superior courts consider so and the events in lower courts brings judges' certainty of history and women's role in courts into question. Everyday magistrates and justices dealt with misdemeanours or more serious crimes in a legal system where women were not only defendants, but also witnesses to murder and manslaughter, and also appeared in crimes of sexual violence committed against them. How their testimony was valued is another matter: Magna Carta's cap. 54 specifically ruled out arrest or imprisonment 'upon the appeal of a woman' for anyone's death except her husband's, affirming women's suspect credibility. Centuries after Magna Carta, women's credibility remained dependent upon status and character, linked directly to gender, hence the marital status questions to women, whatever the role.[17]

Yet whatever lay in the past, Neaves was right: Magna Carta did not apply for, during his time, women participated as all-woman jurors and not otherwise. His reticence in naming the jury of a 'limited kind' ('matrons' or 'pregnancy jury') showed Neaves' discomfort about

DOI: 10.1057/9781137562357.0005

women's bodies, perhaps coupled with apprehension that female plaintiffs (particularly unmarried women) might find offence in 'women's matters'. All-women juries confirmed whether a woman was truthful if, once convicted, she pleaded pregnancy. Women from the community, often from the public gallery, were called to inspect defendants privately, questioning, poking, prodding, and doing whatever else could assist a finding. If 'yes', the woman escaped hanging pending the putative child's birth. Potentially, she could escape hanging altogether. At Thompson's execution, much blood gushing when her body fell raised speculation of her suffering a miscarriage. Conducting the autopsy, pathologist Bernard Spillsbury so concluded. If correct, Thompson would have been entitled to a jury of women and suspension of sentence. She did not request it.[18]

A blunt principle founded arguments against women's jury participation: women were not 'fitted' for public offices and ought not to fill them. In *Olive v. Ingram* (1738), counsel for the (male) plaintiff resorted to Magna Carta, asserting women could appear in court only through a husband; hence, women were 'incapacitated' for any public role, including jury service. Counsel for the (female) defendant asserted a difference between 'an excuse from acting [and] an incapacity of doing so'. This did not help. In *Chorlton v. Lings* (1868–1869) counsel argued public office was 'a burden, not a privilege', excluding women from voting and standing for public office, and so juries. This was a common excuse for women's exclusion.[19] Bebb's counsel in *Bebb v. Law Society* [1914] noted Pollock and Maitland's *History of English Law* (1895) contention that women were on men's level in private rights, however:

> [P]ublic functions have they none. In the camp, at the council board, on the bench, in the jury box there is no place for them.[20]

When the Sex Disqualification (Removal) Act 1919 gave British women a formal right to sit on juries, the 'duty' versus 'right' distinction remained. In *Viscountess Rhondda's Claim* [1922], Viscount Haldane was 'for' her right to join the House of Lords whereas Viscount Birkenhead was 'against', referring to the Act's wording describing jury service as a liability, not a right. Underneath lay a notion of the work being unpalatable, as the London Sessions' juror exclaimed to the *Manchester Guardian* journalist – though affirming it was no reason for not serving. In the US, an Illinois legislator confirmed this widely held prejudice, asserting 'good women don't want to serve in juries' in courtrooms awash with 'vile language': 'Do you want your mothers and sisters in that situation?' In southern states like Mississippi and

DOI: 10.1057/9781137562357.0005

South Carolina, an additional complication existed: prejudice generated apprehension at 'white' women being seated with African American women on juries or rubbing shoulders with African American men. Prominent in the struggle, African American women were not deterred.[21] Some US judges did, however, extend the right (and duty) to women. When in 1869 Wyoming women won the right to vote, women sat on juries from 1870 to 1871. In *The U.S. Women's Jury Movements*, Holly McCammon lists John Howe, CJ's rationale as both conventional (women 'would have a civilizing effect… in the courtroom [and] on the frontier more generally') and tending towards feminism ('women [should have] great power in their dealings with men'). Lawyers and Howe's successor disagreed: defence counsel removed prospective women jurors through peremptory challenges, and upon Howe's retirement, the incoming chief justice abandoned the practice. Jury rights reportedly caused more dissent than enfranchisement.[22]

When in 1920 the 19th Amendment extended the franchise to women, jury pools coming from electoral rolls meant some US courts interpreted this as granting women jury rights. Challenges were lost in *Palmer v. State of Indiana* (1926) and *State of Iowa v. Walker* (1921), affirming that with winning the right to vote, women simultaneously won the right to jury service, and in *Thatcher v. Penn., Ohio, & Detroit Rd Co.* (1928), where compensation for appropriating property being judged by 'a jury of twelve men', 'men' was held to be used generically. In other states, women ran campaigns for years (sometimes shorter, sometimes longer) before legislatures or courts acceded to their claim.

Just as Magna Carta barons claimed a right to trial by peers, along with UK and North American women, antipodean women saw jury service as a right and civic duty, too – asserting their exclusion as wrong on both grounds. Yet recognition that 'the vote' won women 'the jury' was uncommon. From at least the late 19th century Australian women campaigned, but jury rights came long after rights to vote and (often) standing for Parliament. Queensland was first to grant women jury rights in 1923. For Aotearoa/New Zealand, women won jury rights in 1942. Still, this was some twenty years before the last state in the US, Mississippi, recognised women's jury rights in 1968. Similarly in Canada, jury rights were late in coming. In *Edwards v. AG of Canada* [1929], the Privy Council mentioned juries. Saying Roman law had demoted women into subservience, Lord Sankey, LC noted *Coke's Institutes* (1628) asserting women's common law exclusion from being judges or jurors,

DOI: 10.1057/9781137562357.0005

'with the single exception of inquiries by a jury of matrons' (the 'pregnancy jury'). Yet despite Canadian women's recognition as persons and women of the West spearheading this change, women of the North West Territories were precluded from jury service until 1965, with all women (ending ethnicity/race-based discrimination) gaining the right in 1971.[23]

Another battle loomed, however. In North America, the UK, Aotearoa/ New Zealand and Australia, women had an automatic exemption, simply because of their sex. In *Ballard v. United States* (1946) the Supreme Court held that women and men were entitled to serve on federal juries in the same capacity. However, in *Hoyt v. Florida* (1961) a law automatically including men's names for jury service and requiring women to volunteer was affirmed. Not until the 20th century's second half did women gain equal rights with men. The US Supreme Court in *Taylor v. Louisiana* (1975) determined women and men should serve equally, without special exemptions for women. In Canada, the Jury Act 1991 confirmed this, with section 626 of the Canadian Criminal Code saying no person can be disqualified, exempted or excused on grounds of sex. In Australia, criminal law generally being governed by state legislatures, women waged 'state by state' campaigns for jury rights. For example, Western Australia's 1957 Juries Act enabled women to serve, but to claim an absolute exemption on sex grounds. Amendments in 1984 ruled out the sex exemption absolutely.[24]

Jury entitlements are not, however, sufficient. How to exercise the right? Current Comment (1982) notes Australian appeals against systematic challenges eliminating women and Indigenous Australians – deliberately – from juries. In the US, until *JEB v. Alabama* (1994), peremptory challenges against women and African Americans skewed jury make-up. In Canada, defendants have contested jury imbalance on race/ethnicity grounds and poor – or over – representation of women. *R. v. Napoose (No 1)* (1991) and *R. v. Catizone* (1972) successfully challenged array-process irregularities. In *Napoose*, the jury list comprised a ratio of 2:5 favouring male candidates. In *Catizone*, the possible jurors list named three women only. In Canada, however, section 670 of the Criminal Code now provides this cannot found an appeal.[25]

The lawful judgment of peers

Hale believed in witches. He also believed women falsely allege rape and this perspectives still features in courtrooms. Belief systems surrounding

DOI: 10.1057/9781137562357.0005

juries render sexual offences problematic. Once women became eligible for jury service, a defence culture kept women on rape trial juries, women being seen as likely to acquit, through sympathy for defendants, wariness about victim/survivors' antecedents, or both.

In *The American Jury*, Harry Kalven Jnr and Hans Zeisel researched jury trials, questioning fifty-five judges on judge and jury perceptions of guilt. Judges agreed 75–80% of the time with jury verdicts. Rape created the greatest disparity. Judges disagreed with jury acquittals, saying evidence of victim/survivors' prior drinking, single parenthood, frequenting bars alone, dress and demeanour wrongly influenced the verdict, raising the question why judges allowed the irrelevant evidence in, at all.[26] The findings appeared to support defence beliefs of women harshly judging women, contradicting the *Manchester Guardian* woman juror's notion that women on juries would ensure 'greater care' in cases involving women.

Contentions that, confronted with rape, women jurors avoided their own vulnerability by believing only women 'of a type' could suffer the crime (victim-blaming), so concluding 'no crime here' may have had some validity. However, campaigns have wrought change: 1990s' juries appeared more likely to get it right than judges.[27] Now, defence counsel culture may challenge women as prospective rape trial jurors. In 1995, Canadian judges considered this.[28]

In *R. v. Biddle* [1995], identity was disputed. Two separate attacks on women led to Mr Biddle's convictions: assault causing bodily harm and choking with intent to commit an indictable offence. Crown counsel empanelled an all-female jury. One of three appeal points was, was it an abuse of jury selection process, creating a reasonable apprehension of bias? Unconstitutionality of the jury 'stand-by' provision favouring Crown jury selection was determined in *R. v. Bain* [1992], after the *Biddle* trial. Six judges, deciding Biddle's right to appeal on other grounds, avoided the jury bias question. L'Heureux-Dube, Gonthier and McLachlin, JJ addressed it.

Refusing the appeal, in her lone dissent, L'Heureux-Dube, agreeing with McLachlin on the jury question, adopted the appellate court's finding of no reasonable apprehension of jury bias. That women 'may be particularly sensitive to the plight of victims' would not prevent an all-female jury from assessing objectively reliability of identification evidence provided by victim/survivors. It was wrong, too, to assume that the 'reasonable, well-informed observer' would 'reasonably

DOI: 10.1057/9781137562357.0005

apprehend' that an all-woman jury 'would be favourably disposed' to upholding the Crown on identification. Trial counsel made no objection during jury selection, apparently perceiving no bias. Therefore, making 'findings of partiality' on 'assumed stereotypical reactions based on gender' is 'dangerous and contrary to our concepts of equality and individuality'.[29]

Nonetheless, Gonthier said an apparent prosecution attempt 'to modify composition of the jury ... to exclude representativeness ... undermines' jury impartiality. McLachlin disagreed. Representativeness is a standard 'impossible to achieve', she said. The community 'can be divided into a hundred different groups' according to gender, race, class and education:

> Must every group be represented on every jury? If not, which groups are to be chosen and on what grounds? ...

Agreeing that a jury 'must be impartial and competent', she noted the law 'has never suggested ... a jury must be representative':

> For hundreds of years, juries ... were composed entirely of men. Are we to say that all these juries were for that reason partial and incompetent?

Although the meaning of 'jury' has changed over time, these hundreds of years extended from before and after Magna Carta, in Britain for up to 700 years and more. Magna Carta's insistence on 'trial by peers' was emphatic. Not only does it appear in cap. 39, but cap. 21 avows (with other amercement provisions similarly):

> Earls and barons shall be amerced only by their peers and in proportion to the gravity of their offence.

So women lost out, none being a freeman. So, too, noble women: being neither earls nor barons, they had no place on juries, no right to trial by jury of their peers. Gaining this Magna Carta right took women centuries. Yet, as *R. v. Biddle* (1995) shows, women's participation as equals on juries remains problematic, at least for some. For centuries, women appeared – whether as defendants, principal witnesses, witnesses or in other roles – before juries comprised solely of men. Where were the male voices raised for women in drafting Magna Carta? Indeed, why were there no women amongst those drafters, so that Magna Carta was drafted by their peers?

DOI: 10.1057/9781137562357.0005

Notes

1   Holt, *Magna Carta*, 2015, p. 89.
2   Young, *Trial of Frederick Bywaters*, 1923, p. 8; following quotations this source, p. 8.
3   Jesse, *A Pin to see the Peepshow*, 1934, 1979, p. 353.
4   Citing Beattie, *Crime and the Courts*, 1986; Palk, *Gender, Crime, and Judicial Discretion*, 2006; Langbein, 'Shaping the ... criminal trial', 1983; and King, *Crime, Justice, and Discretion*, 2000.
5   Gibson, *What Are You?*, 2013, p. 13; following quotations this source, pp. 19–20.
6   A Woman Correspondent, 1921.
7   Pizan, *The Book of the City*, 1405, 1999, pp. 29–30.
8   Cam, *The Hundred and the Hundred Rolls*, 1963, p. 137; following quotations this source, pp. 184, 186.
9   Reis, *Damned Witches*, 1997; Sharpe, 'Hopkins, Matthew', 2004.
10 Carpenter, *Magna Carta*, 2015, pp. 22–44.
11 Hopkins killed or ordered killing of at least 300 women over a few years: Sharpe, 'Hopkins, Matthew', 2004.
12 Holdsworth, 'Sir Matthew Hale', 1923, p. 407. Acknowledging Holdsworth's 'omissions' today is no relief to women affected by his supporting Hale's misogyny.
13 Geis and Bunn, *A Trial of Witches*, 1997; Notestein, *A History of Witchcraft*, 2003; Wright and Wright, *Witches in and around Suffolk*, 2005.
14 *A Tryal of Witches*, 1682, pp. 55–56.
15 Holdsworth, 'Sir Mathew Hale', 1923.
16 McCammon, *The U.S. Women's Jury Movements*, 2012, pp. 1, 37.
17 *Jex-Blake v. Senatus of University of Edinburgh* (1873), at 832; Gibson, *What Are You?*, 2013.
18 'Edith Thompson', *Capital Punishment*, UK.
19 *Olive v. Ingram* (1738), at 271, 272; *Chorlton v. Lings* (1868–1869), at 376.
20 *Bebb v. Law Society* [1914], at 287.
21 *Viscountess Rhondda's Claim* [1922], at 374, 381; McCammon, *The U.S. Women's Jury Movements*, 2012, pp. 64, 165.
22 McCammon, *The U.S. Women's Jury Movements*, 2014, p. 39; Flexner, *Century of Struggle*, 1959, reprint 1996; Weisbrot, 'Barred from the Bar', 1977, p. 485.
23 Australian Government, 'Women in Australian Society'; 'Woman Juror', 1943; Wilson, 'Nation and government', 2015; *Edwards v. AG of Canada* [1929], at 125, citing Coke, 2 Inst. 119, 3 B1. Comm. 362; North West Territories HRC, *Celebrating 100 Years*.

DOI: 10.1057/9781137562357.0005

24 Heritage Newfoundland and Labrador, *The Modern Women's Movement*; Law Reform Commission, WA, *Selection, Eligibility*; Auty and Toussaint (eds), *A Jury of Whose Peers?* 2004.
25 Current Comment, 'Trial by a Jury?' 1982; Balfour, *The Jury*, 1998, paras 2–11.
26 'Rape shield' statutes now exist in common law countries: Scutt, *Rape Law Reform*, 1980.
27 Scutt, *The Incredible Woman*, 1996.
28 *R. v. Biddle* [1995] CanLII 134 (SCC); also *R. v. Kokopenace* (2015) SCC 28 (CanLII) – on jurors' race/ethnicity.
29 *R. v. Biddle* [1995], adopting Doherty JA (at 770), at 20; following quotations this source, at 18.

DOI: 10.1057/9781137562357.0005

4

Can Women Be Householders?

Abstract: *Magna Carta said widows could stay in their husbands' (sic) houses for forty days after his death. That marital homes belonged equally to widows lacked recognition in law. On marriage, Blackstone's coverture doctrine 'husbands and wives are one' meant wives' property and income belonged to husbands. Noting 'a man's home is his castle', Scutt recounts Canadian, US, UK, Aotearoa/New Zealand and Australian women's campaigns for Matrimonial Property Acts, for property ownership and income rights, and for recognition of the economic value of women's unpaid contributions to marital assets as equal to men's monetary contributions. Scutt points out that on marital breakdown, men's contributions to property continue to be seen as greater than women's, stereotyping of women and women's traditional role influencing judges' assessments of contributions.*

Keywords: Blackstone and coverture; husband and wife are 'one'; law of coverture; Matrimonial Property Acts; women and income rights; women and property rights; women's property rights campaigns

Scutt, Jocelynne A. *Women and Magna Carta: A Treaty for Rights or Wrongs?* Basingstoke: Palgrave Macmillan, 2016. DOI: 10.1057/9781137562357.0006.

DOI: 10.1057/9781137562357.0006

> A widow, after the death of her husband ... may remain in the house
> of her husband for forty days after his death, within which time her
> dower shall be assigned to her.
>
> *Magna Carta, cap. 7*

Who owns what

One of the most contradictory English language oaths underpins the
traditional marriage ceremony. The 1879 version of the US *Common Book
of Prayer*, replicated throughout the Western world, says:

> WITH this Ring I thee wed, and with all my worldly goods I thee endow: In
> the Name of the Father, and of the Son, and of the Holy Ghost. Amen.

Coming from the putative husband's lips, precisely the opposite is true.
Historically, the woman, as wife, bestowed all her worldly goods upon
the husband. Even upon betrothal, a woman lost control of her property.
Her husband could reclaim any property she gave away before marrying,
including real property, goods, chattels and income. During the 19th and
20th centuries women waged a struggle for property rights and autonomy over their earnings. This struggle had its roots and necessity in the
society and culture spawning Magna Carta.[1]

Albeit acknowledging women had fewer rights than men, Carpenter,
in *Magna Carta*, says 'women did have rights over property'. But the
description of property a woman might 'own' as 'the house of her
husband' – even when he's dead – highlights the reality. Confirming
again male preeminence in the property stakes, cap. 26 made another
concession. Where a lay fee was held in favour of the king, the king's
sheriff or bailiff could seize and remove chattels to its value. The residue
went to a deceased's estate, apart from a portion reserved for his wife
and children 'in their reasonable shares'; if nothing were owed, all property would go to them. True, then, widows and wives rate a mention. Yet
property – inherited, gifted or earned – was 'his'. According to Magna
Carta, women lived in their husbands' homes, in and on their property,
widows' rights extending to forty days only. All chattels belonged to the
husband, whatever contribution a wife made. On marriage, real property belonged to him, so long as he lived, and to his heirs when dead.
A widow could claim her dower – but had to pay to do so, for it was

DOI: 10.1057/9781137562357.0006

claimed from *his* property. She could lay claim to some chattels – but not determine what was 'reasonable'.

Referring to women plaintiffs in suits involving land (although most appeared with a male relative), Holt's *Magna Carta* gives examples of a widow asserting authority over her dead husband's vassals, and one regaining her dead husband's will, taken (wrongly) by King John.[2] However, Ranulf de Glanville's 1780 *Treatise on the Law and Customs of the Kingdom of England* confirms property law disadvantaged women. Unlike heirs, an unmarried heiress, even having reached her majority on her father's death, could not assume her inheritance. She being a ward, her lord was entitled to marry her off to whomever he chose. If her lord were the king, he held this privilege. Being female, she could not inherit until she married. Once married, the property devolved to her husband. Magna Carta protected heirs from ill-suited marriage: cap. 6 provided heirs should be married 'without disparagement', ending the king's practice of linking heirs with wives of lesser standing. Heiresses gained no protection, the king still able to use them to seal his alliances by promoting lowly men into higher positions.

Pressing John over Magna Carta, barons wished to consolidate their own dynasties. The five articles immediately preceding that addressing widows' forty-day rights tackle rights of heirs of earls, barons or those holding from the king in chief by knight service. Upon death of an earl or baron, an heir having reached his majority will pay the king £100 only to secure succession to the land, whilst a knight's heirs must pay no more than 100s. Underage heirs pay nothing, their guardians required to care for the estate, maintaining all houses, fish ponds, ponds and mills for reasonable payment, ensuring the land and everything on it passes in good order to the heir once reaching his majority.

In 1216, widows' forty-day rights were clarified. Henry III's Magna Carta denied widows any right to remain in castles. This prohibition continued in Henry's 1225 Magna Carta and versions promulgated by later kings. No reference to 'widows' husbands' castles' appeared: presumably a castle being such a masculine construction and concept, its male ownership required no statement, providing another dimension to Coke's well-known 1604 *Semayne's Case* edict, that a man's home 'is his castle'.

Magna Carta did provide a benefit to potentially independent women. During forty days after her husband's death, a widow's dower would be assigned to her – without any debts the husband might have 'to the Jews'

DOI: 10.1057/9781137562357.0006

or others being paid from it. Thus women in this class, at least, were not penniless upon a husband's death (though 'the Jews' and others lost out). Further, the king forfeited his right to press widows into marriage, by which he (and his forebears) had formed alliances promoting their own interests. King John thus promoted William Marshall, who in turn supported him through Magna Carta travails and, as regent to Henry III on John's death, protected the Angevin line.[3]

Before Magna Carta, a widow could evade by paying the king: eschewing marriage with Walter of Tew, Avelina, Osbert de Longchamps' widow, paid 500 marks. Walter paid 400 marks only.[4] Under Magna Carta, Avelina would pay nothing. Still, widows did not escape altogether. So long as wishing to live without a husband, no widow could be distrained to marry. Widows had striven for this goal 'over the past generation', Holt observes; nonetheless, under cap. 8 a widow must give security 'not [to] marry without our assent ...'.[5] And as Carpenter's *Magna Carta* acknowledges, surely Magna Carta's favouring widows 'owed a good deal' to male relatives' demands:

> No son wanted to see his mother, with all her lands, taken off by some second husband. It was far better ... she remain single, [so] the son ... might hope to profit ...[6]

At the same time, 12th- and 13th-century women were no mere pawns in men's hands. Like Holt, Carpenter notes they had, before 1215, 'been active in securing, in return for money, precisely the kinds of concessions they [obtained] in Magna Carta'. In this, Magna Carta anticipated 20th-century struggles to ensure widows were not left in a property and income-less limbo immediately after a husband's death.

Requiring assessment of a deceased person's property to determine payment of probate or inheritance tax, 20th-century laws disadvantaged women. Even after Married Women's Property Acts, husbands' names frequently appeared on all or most property documents without acknowledging wives as contributors and, hence, properly equal owners. All property bearing the husband's name was ensnared in administration pending assessment and payment of tax, before a widow could access it. In the late 20th-century, marital homes were more frequently registered in joint names, the surviving spouse (wife or husband) automatically gaining full ownership. However, where the state held in abeyance all other property – including income earning real property, shares, superannuation and the like – until probate was granted, a woman could be left in a mortgaged

DOI: 10.1057/9781137562357.0006

home without mortgage payments or money for grocery or utility bills. If the marital home was in the husband's name alone – as with homes devolving to servicemen, a post–Second World War practice – a widow could be left pining for Magna Carta's forty days of grace.

During the 1970s, rising inflation meant even modest estates were trapped for lengthy periods in probate and administration.[7] Where a husband left a will, widows remained in limbo pending grant of probate and distribution of assets. Where husbands died intestate, widows could wait months for settling estate finances. Di Graham of Women's Electoral Lobby (WEL) Probate Action Group ran a major Australian campaign addressing this iniquity, compounded because on marriage many women left paid employment when raising children, becoming 'at least ... "temporary paupers" on the husband's death':

> Despite having served as 'unpaid housekeepers' for perhaps forty years they may well have to sell the family home to pay the death duties, unless they could prove they had paid for at least half from their own income.[8]

That women pushed or lulled into 'enforced economic dependence' or having 'dutifully stayed home from work' were temporarily trapped was ignored by legislators and bureaucrats alike. WEL's lobbying resulted in abolition of probate between husbands and wives. Unfortunately, although Graham argued inheritance taxes should be increased across the board to maintain government revenues, governments abolished probate all together. Although widows were better off, society as a whole lost out through a decrease in governments' capacity to provide public services for which widows had paid disproportionately.

Women's property rights – recognising ownership

Wollstonecraft saw property as a thorn in the side of humanity. In *A Vindication* (1792) she upbraided inherited wealth as underpinning class difference and promoting idleness. Wanting 'more equality in society', almost 600 years after Magna Carta, she demanded an end to women's man-made dependence:

> Whilst they are absolutely dependent on their husbands [women] will be cunning, mean, and selfish ... [9]

Less than a century later, Coventry Patmore was idealising his wife, Emily, as 'The Angel in the House' (1891) – the precise position from which Wollstonecraft sought to relieve women, and the precise opposite of the harridan into which (Wollstonecraft feared) every woman would devolve, in following the Patmore ideal. For Patmore, at least in the first days of marriage ('Sweet Stranger, now my three days' Wife …'), paying for an article of his wife's dress is an amusing affirmation of their troth:

> I, while the shop-girl fitted on
> The sand-shoes, look'd where, down the bay,
> The sea glow'd with a shrouded sun.
> 'I'm ready, Felix; will you pay?'[10]

Politically active women agreed with Wollstonecraft. So long as 'husband and wife were one', women's independence was unattainable – and property lay at the heart of the matter.

From the mid-19th century, women's activism ensured common law legislatures in Britain, North America, Australia and Aotearoa/New Zealand passed Married Women's Property Acts affirming women's ownership of property they brought into marriage and income earned during marriage. This was essential to redress denial of women's autonomy under Blackstone's (1765) law of coverture: 'that one is the husband'.[11]

In 1848 New York led with its Married Women's Property Act declaring that real and personal property 'of any female who may hereafter marry' owned by her at the time of marriage:

> … shall not be subject to the disposal of her husband, nor be liable for his debts, and shall continue her sole and separate property, as if she were a single female.[12]

'For the effectual protection of the property of married women', the Act covered already married women in identical terms, except her property remained liable for her husband's debts contracted up to the date of its enactment. Furthermore, any 'married female' could lawfully receive, 'by gift, grant, devise or bequest' both real and personal property, and 'rents, issues and profits thereof', from 'any person other than her husband' for her 'sole and separate use as if she were a single female'. Such property was protected from her husband's disposal and avoided liability for his debts.

Other states followed.

Nonetheless, courts undermined the laws. Illinois passed its Married Woman's Property Act in 1861. In 1869 in *Cole v. Van Riper* the Illinois

DOI: 10.1057/9781137562357.0006

Supreme Court addressed it. Denying, at that time, Myra Bradwell the right to enter legal practice (allegedly to protect woman's 'natural born "femininity"' from destruction through the 'strife' of the Bar) little surprise that married women's property rights were interpreted narrowly. In *Van Riper*, the statute was held not to give a wife power to convey her real estate without her husband's consent, manifested through his jointly signing the deed. This followed because, the judges said, the husband's tenancy by courtesy after his wife's death was left unimpaired.[13]

Delivered by Lawrence, CJ the joint judgment said a literal interpretation of the Act was impossible. It would mean a wife could keep her husband out of the house if it belonged to her alone. With personal property, he would have no right to take a book from the shelf or sit in any chair other than that she prescribed. As well as giving a woman a practical right to separate from her husband without legal action, this was 'absurd'. The legislature sought not to 'loosen' matrimonial 'bonds', nor 'create an element of constant strife between husband and wife'. It aimed solely to protect wives 'against the misfortunes, improvidence or possible vice' of husbands, enabling wives to 'withhold ... property from being levied on and sold for the payment of his debts, or squandered by him against her wishes'.

Lacking explicit renunciation of a husband's right of effective ownership of his wife's property after her death, should children be born to the marriage, then that 'right of courtesy' remained. In any event, the New York Act 'provided unambiguously' that a wife had conveyancing power over her own property, yet like Pennsylvania and New Jersey, the Illinois law 'employed terms of ... general character' only. Pennsylvania and New Jersey Supreme Courts agreed. Wives were denied the right to convey their own property in the absence of their husband's consent.

In the UK, Married Women's Property Acts passed in 1870, 1882 and 1893. Claire Jones explains in *The Married Women's Property Acts* that Millicent Fawcett, the Langham Place Group and Kensington Society were reinvigorated in married women's property rights campaigning when Fawcett's purse was 'snatched by a youth in London':

> When the boy's crime was read out in court Fawcett was shocked to hear him charged with stealing a purse ... 'the property of Henry Fawcett' (her husband). She ... recalled ... 'I felt as if I had been charged with theft myself'.[14]

The 1870 Act gave women the right to own their own income: moneys they earned would no longer be their husband's property. Following the

DOI: 10.1057/9781137562357.0006

New York approach, in 1882 married women gained rights over their property akin to single women. However, not until 1893 did the UK adopt the New York provision ensuring married women owned property, including inheritances and gifts, acquired by her *during* marriage.

Constance Backhouse in 'Married Women's Property Law' reports that, following US states' lead, in 1851 the New Brunswick legislature passed the first Canadian statute 'to Secure to Married Women Real and Personal Property Held in Their Own Right'. Not equating married women with unmarried women, the Act concentrated on 'deserted or abandoned' married women, empowering them, in their own name, to sue for debts or damages 'notwithstanding any discharge or release from her husband to the contrary'. In 1869 this was extended to married women living apart from a husband, 'not willfully and of her own accord'. Prince Edward Island followed in 1860, whilst in 1866 Nova Scotia passed its own law, based on the UK Act.[15]

In Australia, the first legislative acknowledgement was the 1879 New South Wales Act, replicating 1870 and 1874 UK Acts. Aotearoa/New Zealand introduced the Married Women's Property Protection Act 1860, replicating UK deserted wives provisions, and the Married Women's Property Act 1884 put married women generally in single women's position vis-à-vis property.[16]

Where covering real property, these initiatives replicated Magna Carta in their relevance to women from families with property holdings to pass to daughters for their sons. Equity already provided mechanisms for landed gentry and aristocracy to secure ancestral holdings upon a daughter's marriage. However, the impetus was not women's rights, but preserving estates for male heirs – not unlike Magna Carta. Yet 19th-century Acts dealing with income had important implications for working-class women, and for middle-class women entering secretarial and administrative positions, and shop-work.

As Sue Bruley recounts in *Women in Britain since 1900*, from 1870 onwards, numbers of women clerks 'rose from 2000 in 1851 to 166,000 in 1911':

> The 'white blouse' revolution … was created from … retail stores, particularly the new large department stores; the civil service and local government; state and private education ….[17]

This followed for Western women generally. Although single women tended to dominate, married women also moved into growth areas of

DOI: 10.1057/9781137562357.0006

paid employment. Both continued working in traditional fields, too – factories outside the home, and household work, as well as taking in lodgers, washing and ironing. At least their earnings were now their own.

Women's property rights – recognising contribution

Henry III's 1217 Magna Carta defined a widow's dower as 'a third of the land her husband held in his lifetime' unless less was agreed at the time of marriage.[18] Dower constituted a widow's lifetime interest in property which, upon her death, went to children of the marriage. This followed whether or not the woman brought property equivalent to, or greater or lesser than, the dower into the marriage. Generally, property – most likely more than the stipulated one-third – did come into the marriage along with the woman. However, that the dower could be greater recognised either that a woman, as a former dependent of her husband, remained so after his death and required financial support; alternatively, that her contribution during marriage *entitled* her to property in her widowhood.

Traditionally, the former not the latter rationale held sway: women viewed as dependent on men for survival and marriage enabling that survival. With Married Women's Property Acts clarifying women's property rights so that what a woman brought to the marriage, whether real or personal property, remained hers, the campaign shifted. Women in the 20th century's latter half sought legislative recognition of women's contribution to marital assets other than simply by earnings or property taken into marriage or acquired during its course. This was closely allied to divorce law reform.

When King John agreed to Magna Carta, marriage had no ending for the 'ordinary' person apart from death or desertion. In the upper echelons, consolidation of property and power through advantageously arranged marriages was standard. Birth of heirs rather than companionate marriage was the principal aim. Inconvenient marriages could be ended by annulment. Ecclesiastical courts ruled over marriage and family disputes, although an uncomfortable alliance could be severed through Parliament by a Bill of Divorcement. Although some gained an annulment or even a Bill, neither was readily available to women, whatever their class.[19]

DOI: 10.1057/9781137562357.0006

As for the lower echelons, parties were not always joined formally in wedlock, although the extent of common law marriage is disputed. Such marriages never were, Rebecca Probert's 'The Myths of History' says, a common or recognised practice in England or Wales, while colonisation brought recognition of common law marriage in some American states (such as Texas) through misreading legal texts.[20] Still, whether formally constituted or not, *Flores v. Flores* (1993) held all marriages required formalities to end them.

The year of Magna Carta, Pope Innocent III declared marriage a sacrament governed wholly by ecclesiastical laws. Nullity was an ecclesiastical invention – for some church-approved reason (perhaps failure to consummate, or impotence) the marriage was no marriage at all. This was not divorce: (theoretically) never having been married, no status existed from which divorce could emanate. Ecclesiastical law recognised separation 'from bed and board' ('divorce *a mensa et thoro*'), parties living apart, but unable to remarry.

In the 19th century, reformist agitation led to marital matters transferring from ecclesiastical to secular courts. In Britain, the Matrimonial Causes Act 1857 commenced in England and Wales on 1 January 1858. In the Probate and Divorce Division, access ostensibly open to all, whether 'high' or 'low' society, marriages could be ended. In 'Creswell', Joshua Getzler reflects on the importance of Creswell, J. as Division head, determinedly ensuring that ecclesiastic principles, generally detrimental to women's interests, no longer held sway. However, the Act's discriminatory provisions, namely a man's entitlement to divorce upon proof of his wife's single act of adultery, while for women adultery as a ground of divorce required special circumstances (such as incest or cruelty – 'adultery plus'), together with family life trends and socio-cultural change, propelled women's organisations into action.[21] As with marital property reforms, protest accompanied recommendations for change.

Like North America, Australia handled divorce initially on a state-by-state basis. Aotearoa/New Zealand provisions were country-wide. Despite some discrepancies in timing, generally divorce laws were consistent with those introduced in the UK, incorporating similar grounds, all involving fault – adultery being the principal ground. Discriminatory provisions – the universally adopted 'adultery plus' – prevailed in Victoria until 1959, other Australian states having eliminated it earlier. That year the federal Matrimonial Causes Act introduced a national scheme of fourteen grounds including adultery, cruelty, attempted murder, serious crimes or repeated

DOI: 10.1057/9781137562357.0006

offences, drunkenness, desertion, and committal to an insane asylum. Some 'fault' grounds were common to other jurisdictions and although appearing neutral in operation were not. *Brown v. Brown* (1976), the last High Court case under this Act, showed a clear anti-woman bias, declaring 'cruelty' required serial acts of violence and refusing Mrs Brown's divorce when, in any event, several acts of violence occurred.[22] Nonetheless, the Act provided for 'no fault' divorce: a five-year separation meant a party could initiate divorce albeit the (former) partner resisted it.

Ten years after Australia's first national law, Canada's Divorce Act 1968 followed, covering all provinces. Then in 1986, a new national law incorporated existing and new grounds, including adultery, mental or physical cruelty, and a reduced separation clause requiring twelve months' living separately and apart.[23]

Today, many common law jurisdictions, including the UK, retain divorce based principally in fault, albeit generally including a ground of separation for a specified period, enabling a party to apply for 'no fault' divorce.[24] In 1970, California introduced a 'no fault' regime akin to Australia under the Family Law Act 1975. Despite controversy stirred by religious institutions and political conservatives, the Australian Act swept away all fault requirements, leaving one ground of divorce: twelve months' separation. For Aotearoa/New Zealand, the Family Proceedings Act 1980 similarly makes separation the sole ground for divorce, albeit expressed as 'irreconcilable differences' with two years being the required period.[25] None of this was presaged by Magna Carta, where the notion of women's rights, much less women's freedom from oppressive marriage, was remote. Equally importantly, the contention that women might by non-financial means and 'women's work' contribute to the accumulation of assets and thereby be entitled to property ownership rights was not contemplated.

Australia's Family Law Act endeavours to recognise the economic value of work traditionally done in families (mainly) by women during marriage. Both during the marriage and upon separation and divorce, principles underpinning 'who owns what' are based on accumulation of assets by:

▸ Direct financial contribution – including mortgage payments, acquisition of shares, monetary payments into a superannuation or pension scheme, etc;
▸ Indirect financial contribution – including utility payments, payments for family holidays, childcare fees, school fees and excursions – enabling a partner to earn, make mortgage payments, etc;

DOI: 10.1057/9781137562357.0006

▸ Direct non-financial contribution – including maintenance and/
or improvements to the family home or other assets by painting,
renovating, landscaping, gardening, etc – so property is improved
or remains sound, its value increasing or not deteriorating;

▸ Indirect non-financial contribution – including childcare, husband
and family care, washing, ironing and washing up – enabling a
partner to earn, make mortgage and superannuation payments,
undertake property improvement and maintenance, etc.

However, the tendency remains that the male partner's paidwork is seen
(whether consciously or unconsciously) as intrinsically more valuable
than the female partner's paidwork, and non-financial contributions
are similarly disparately assessed. Generally, paidwork in traditionally
female industries and professions is valued less – unequal pay a stark
reminder – so judges must make a conscious decision not to be influenced by this downgrading of value when assessing contribution and,
then, division of assets. Similarly, work in the home – whether housework or childcare – is not valued equally with paidwork or even unpaid-
work in the public sphere, particularly when undertaken by men. Lions,
Rotary Club, Kiwanis, Apex Clubs of Australia come to mind, contrasted
against Zonta, Soroptimists, Professional & Business Women's Clubs.

As Fogarty, J. said in *Waters and Jurek* (1995), partners in most
marriages inhabit roles, sharing duties and responsibilities with certain
duties and responsibilities falling on one, different duties and responsibilities devolving to the other.[26] The Family Law Act intended to acknowledge this by giving equal value to all duties and responsibilities so that,
in crude though realistic terms, if one partner devoted a major part of
their time and energies to raising the children, whilst the other spent a
major part of their time and energies in accumulating property through
earning money, the latter should be seen as an equal contribution to the
former and vice versa. Yet 'the ways of the world' intrude and the notion
that earning money is more important than caring for children influ-
ences how contributions are measured.

Marriage and Magna Carta

No woman's name appears in Magna Carta. It contains no woman's
signature. Yet in addition to King John, twenty-seven men are named
parties. On 15 June 1215, Runnymede was a male enclave. The division of

DOI: 10.1057/9781137562357.0006

labour at Runnymede is not so stark today. Yet land remains dominated by male ownership, with property held mainly in male hands. Marriage under Magna Carta followed this pattern, with repercussions today. Eight hundred years on, the division of labour at Runnymede is not extinct.

This division of labour – which continues, however much talk of women and men sharing childcare and housework 'equally'[27] – impacts on life during and after marriage. Fogarty recognised this, in addressing post-divorce capacities and opportunities, when both 'partnership and division of roles and responsibilities … come to an end', parties remaining without the partnership but with the roles:

> [T]he world outside the marriage does not recognise some of the activities that within the marriage [once were] regarded as valuable contributions … Post separation the party who … assumed the less financially rewarded [marriage] responsibility … is at an immediate disadvantage. Yet that party often cannot simply turn to more financially rewarding activities. Often, opportunities … are no longer open, or, if they are, time is required before they can be assessed and acted upon.[28]

Assessments of future 'needs' as a criterion for assets division is supposed to overcome this. However, bias towards direct financial contribution and gender is confirmed in common law development of a principle, now abandoned in Australia, that 'special contribution' is rewarded with a greater share of assets on divorce. 'Special' contribution encompasses the acumen of a 'good' business person or entrepreneur, skills of a successful artist or specialist surgeon, or an inheritance. Women are most likely to be able to qualify only in the latter category. Yes, there are brilliant women artists and entrepreneurs, skilled surgeons and successful businesswomen. However, they are not as frequently acknowledged as men in those categories, and opportunities for admission to 'special' classifications are fewer. Notably, references to brilliant homemakers, exceptional mothering skills, skilled housework are lacking. Occasional reference to 'good parenting' does not qualify for the asset allocation associated with 'good business acumen'.[29]

Brilliant women were not non-existent in 1215, but none was present at Runnymede. In 2015 brilliant women abound, too. The problem lies with the notion that skills and abilities attributed to women are invisible or, if seen, are more often classed 'ordinary', meaning (as with Magna Carta) family and property law do not yet recognise women as equals.

DOI: 10.1057/9781137562357.0006

Notes

1   Scutt and Graham, *For Richer, For Poorer*, 1984.
2   Holt, *Magna Carta*, 2015, pp. 164,181, 323.
3   Carpenter, *Magna Carta*, 2015, pp. 101, 103, 410; Starke, *Magna Carta*, 2015.
4   Carpenter, *Magna Carta*, 2015, p. 215.
5   Magna Carta, cap. 8; Holt, *Magna Carta*, 2015, p. 22.
6   Carpenter, *Magna Carta*, 2015, p. 105; following quotation is also by Carpenter.
7   Bryan, 'The Great Inflation', 2013.
8   See Scutt, 'Fair Shares', 1994, pp. 32–33; Sawer and Radford, *Making Women Count*, 2008.
9   Wollstonecraft, *A Vindication*, 1792, 1975, 2004, p. 91.
10 Patmore, *The Angel*, 1891, p. 186.
11 Blackstone, *Commentaries*, 1765.
12 *Married Women's Property Act* 1848 (NY), s. 1; Law Library of Congress, 'Married Women's Property Laws'; Chused, 'Married Women's Property Law', 1983; Wilson, *Law, Gender, and Injustice,* 1991.
13 *Cole v. Van Riper* (1861); following quotations that case, at 481, 482–483; also *Walker v. Beamy*; *Naylor v. Field*.
14 Jones, 'The Married Women's Property Acts', 2012; Sachs and Wilson, *Sexism and the Law*, 1978, Pt 2, 'Judges and Genders', p. 136ff; Holcombe, *Wives and Property*, 1983; Shanley, *Feminism, Marriage*, 1989.
15 Backhouse, 'Married Women's Property Law', 1988; Bradbury (ed.), *Canadian Family History*, 1992.
16 Scutt, *Women and the Law*, 1990, pp. 205–206; Scutt and Graham, *For Richer, For Poorer*, 1984; McLintock, *An Encyclopaedia*, 1966.
17 Bruley, *Women in Britain*, 1999, p. 29, citing Zimmeck, 'Jobs for the girl' in John (ed.), *Unequal Opportunities*, 1986.
18 Carpenter, *Magna Carta*, p. 413; Brand, ' "Deserving" and "undeserving" wives', 2001.
19 See Getzler, 'Cresswell', 2004, 2009.
20 Probert, 'The Myths', 2013; also Lind, *Common Law Marriage*, 2008.
21 D'Cruz, 'Women and the family' in Purvis (ed.), *Women's History*, 1995, pp. 51–84.
22 *Brown v. Brown* (1976); Scutt, 'Murphy and family law', 1986.
23 Jordan, 'The Federal Divorce Act', 1968.
24 Bowcott, 'No-fault divorces', 2012, reports England and Wales 'most senior family law judge' saying 'couples should be granted a quick legal separate without shame'.
25 Phillips, *Divorce in New Zealand*, 1981.
26 Parkinson, 'Quantifying the homemaker contribution', 2003.

DOI: 10.1057/9781137562357.0006

27 Craig and Sawrikar, 'Housework and divorce', 2007; Treas and Drobnic (eds), *Dividing the Domestic*, 2010; Bittman, *Juggling Time*, 1991.

28 *Waters and Jurek* (1995), at 82,379.

29 Australia: *Kane and Kane* [2013]. 'Special contribution' UK: *Charman v. Charman* [2007]; also Sendall, *Family Law Handbook*, 2015; Probert, *Family Law*, 2011.

DOI: 10.1057/9781137562357.0006

5

Access to Law and Justice

Abstract: *By Magna Carta, 'no one' would be sold, refused or delayed right or justice. Blackstone's coverture doctrine denied wives justice, disadvantaging single women, too. Matrimonial Causes Acts meant UK, US, Canadian, Aotearoa/New Zealand and Australian women gained property rights and obligations. As Scutt explains, women wanting loans or credit purchasers had to find male guarantors, yet women were easily persuaded to repay defaulting husbands' loans. Hence, banks valued wives, taking advantage when women's signatures became important. Women sought justice for release from financial transactions not explained to them. Some courts constructed 'special' laws for wives. Scutt challenges courts' understandings of women, wives and justice. Women, Scutt observes, must challenge sexist government policies too, like the UK Fawcett Society in 2010, seeking justice through judicial review.*

Keywords: judicial review of 2010 UK budget; Fawcett Society's 2010 judicial review action; wives signing documents; women and guarantees; women and guarantors; women and sureties; women's access to justice; women's access to law; women's rights to credit

Scutt, Jocelynne A. *Women and Magna Carta: A Treaty for Rights or Wrongs?* Basingstoke: Palgrave Macmillan, 2016. DOI: 10.1057/9781137562357.0007.

> To no one will we sell, to no one will we refuse or delay, right or justice.
>
> *Magna Carta, cap. 40*

Neutrality, is thy name justice?

Representation, seizing land, and marrying off heirs and widows did not alone exercise Runnymede barons' minds. Challenging government via the king's caprices, they sought more accessible, better administered, efficient and fair justice. Did they envisage women making independent claims, being represented in courts, receiving speedy justice, or being treated fairly and equally at law? Here, Magna Carta language was gender neutral. In outlawing the right to sell, refuse or delay justice, did Magna Carta ensure women rights to legal remedies?

Justice is depicted blindfolded, scales in one hand weighing claims, a sword in the other. This implies neutrality and fairness are dispensed only by ignoring litigants' characteristics, background or features. Criminal justice critiques say otherwise: neutrality is impossible, honoured only in the breach. As for civil justice, blindness to sex or gender, race or ethnicity, class or status, or disability and other identities or attributes can compound, not ameliorate, injustice.

Just as King John's decisions affected barons, today government's decisions affect women. Judicial review scrutinises government decision-making: decision-makers must disregard irrelevant considerations, taking account of relevant considerations only. Hence, if a government budget slashes services mainly affecting women and women's jobs, then as in *R. (On the Application of the Fawcett Society) v. Chancellor of the Exchequer* [2010] women need judicial review to make their case. Discrimination law demands justice similarly. In *Fares v. Box Hill College of TAFE and Anor* (1992), Katje Fares' claim was that her ethnicity and sex/gender underpinned her negative treatment as an instructor in clothing trade practice and theory.[1] In *Leves v. Haines* (1986), Melinda Leves sought a remedy against sex/gender discrimination when she, at an all-girls government school, was denied the opportunity to study computer management, there being insufficient computers and no classes. Her twin brother, Rhys, at an all-boys government school, studied technical drawing and computer management, his school giving them high priority and

DOI: 10.1057/9781137562357.0007

students having daily computer access. Asserting it was 'too expensive' to do this at Melinda Leves' school, the New South Wales Minister for Education suggested domestic science as an alternative. Confronting sex/gender assumptions and stereotyping of girls educational preferences, rights and needs was essential to a just outcome.[2]

So, too, with outcomes based implicitly in particular attributes or identities: the law must ensure rules and regulations, penalties and privileges, punishments and rewards are not framed according to prejudice, bias or self-interest.

Magna Carta ostensibly ensured widows freedom from coercive marriage. Superficially, this prioritised rights for which widows had fought for a generation.[3] Yet it hid sons' expectations of inheritance and disguised the interests of men not yet dead, seeking to protect their lands from the grave. Magna Carta advanced women's interests where male kin required a remedy. Defiantly reading women 'in' to Magna Carta, or calling for a justice it should advance anyway, with Holt's backing for its adaptability through repeated reinterpretation and as Beloff's 'speaking statute', places women centre-stage.[4]

In *A Vindication* (1792) Wollstonecraft rails against laws making husbands and wives 'an absurd unit', reducing a woman to a 'mere cipher'.[5] Yet despite the law limiting women's capacity for legal action and entrenching social and cultural expectations, some women resisted. Born c1373, Margery Kempe rejected cipher-hood. In *The Book of Margery Kempe* (1438) she describes an exchange with her husband, John Kempe, who makes three requests of her. First, he and she should lie together abed, as once they did. Secondly, she pay his debts before departing for Jerusalem. Thirdly, she eat and drink with him 'on the Fryday as ye wer wont to don'. Margery, in turn, wishes John to cease importuning her, for she wants to remain chaste:

> Sere, yf it lyke yow, ye schal grawnt me my desyr, and ye schal have yowr desyr. Grawntyth me that ye schal not komyn in my bed, and I grawnt yow to qwyte yowr dettys er I go to Jerusalem. And makyth my body fe to God, so that ye nevyr make no chalengyng in me to askyn no dett of matrimony aftyr this day whyl ye levyn, and I schal etyn and drunkyn on the ryday at yowr byddying...[6]

She pays John's debts and achieves her object, her body chaste according to her biblical obedience. Freed to go to Jerusalem, how much eating and drinking with her on Fridays will there be? The story demonstrates

DOI: 10.1057/9781137562357.0007

that despite marriage, Margery held onto some money or knew she retained an equitable estate in property she took into marriage.[7] She exercised independence of movement, too, albeit subject to a trade-off, her Jerusalem pilgrimage predicated on settling Kempe's debts.

Not all women were so fortunate. Some had access to equitable interests, some through trusts, although these generally promoted estate interests for sons and, as Susan Staves writes in *Married Women's Separate Property in England, 1660–1833*, the law was sometimes honoured in the breach.[8] Indeed the nub of Margery Kempe's story is that albeit a traveller and woman able to negotiate with her husband from a position of strength, ultimately she paid her husband's debtors. All too common, even today, women find themselves similarly trapped. Financial dealings can bind women just as much as marital constraints, and marital constraints can ensnare women in financial dealings. Property ownership and income are not the only economic matters affecting women's rights. If she lacked money to settle her husband's debts, would his creditors have pursued her? Would she have had a remedy?[9]

On valuing a signature

Margery Brunham and John Kempe married in about 1393. She was around twenty years old. She paid Kempe's debts in 1413. Maturity may have brought her greater autonomy. Perhaps family circumstances encouraged her greater self-sufficiency than her contemporaries: between 1370 and 1391, her father was mayor of Bishops (now Kings) Lynne; between 1364 and 1384 he was the town's MP six times. John was neither as accomplished as his father-in-law nor his father, 'a successful Lynne merchant'.[10] Yet why, simply because she married him, should Margery Kempe repay a man's independently accrued debts? Since he had rights to rents and charges from her land, an astute creditor might have claimed them, anyway.

Retaining an equitable interest in their property meant married women could borrow money against it in limited circumstances.[11] When, unlike Margery Kempe, they did not have even this limited power, they could not assume a husband's debt. This changed once Married Women's Property Acts recognised married women's separate income rights. Finance and borrowing laws became crucial. So did access to a remedy for unjust treatment.

DOI: 10.1057/9781137562357.0007

Bankers' rapaciousness and money-making strategies drove the 2007–2008 global financial crisis. Banks have not necessarily curtailed that cavalier approach to borrowers today. A history of 'man as income (or property) owner', 'husband as marital partner who counts' underscores the question: is a woman's signature significant to banks – and to her. The past impacts on the present. When laws once denied women their own income and assets, the complex role of money, its place in women's history acute, means women's access to law – securing a remedy – is crucial.

In *The Business of Everyday Life*, Beverly Lemire describes 1830s loan companies providing services for the working-class. The Irish Loan Fund, Cheltenham Loan Society and Hertford-based Aldenham Loan Society anticipated Nobel Prize winning 20th-century micro-credit Grameem Bank. But in 19th-century England and Ireland, these small companies skewed their lending towards working-class men. Single women featured minimally in account books: 22% for the Aldenham Society, dropping progressively over ten years to 14%. Women's marital status (single or widowed) was recorded, with one account alone noting occupation – a widow named as a publican. Loans were small, one woman borrowing her rent, another purchasing a pig. Male borrowers were categorised solely by their work, as labourers, publicans, postmen, shoemakers, bakers, wheelwrights and butchers. Their marital status wasn't mentioned, though wives, often well-known in the area, attended the loans office, ensuring payments were maintained.[12]

Six women were guarantors for male borrowers on Aldenham Society books. All women borrowers had a male guarantor. This, and the bias towards male borrowers, is consistent with 20th-century practices. In the 1960s and 1970s, women faced discrimination by finance companies and banks. Even today, studies find women paying more for a mortgage, while banks and finance providers may remain less willing to finance women's business start-ups or personal loans. In the past, however small the loan or low-cost the purchase, women had to provide a guarantor. Even an unrelated man was better than no one. Lacking a guarantor, women's applications failed, whatever their salary levels. Interrogation by finance companies and banks meant women ran a gamut of intrusive questions about marital and family intentions. Some finance providers required proof of tubal ligation or other irreversible contraception. Australian and US research shows banks and finance providers denying women credit without checking income and assets, refusing them

DOI: 10.1057/9781137562357.0007

credit application forms or requiring a male guarantor, even one earning less. Because the market generally 'rewards' women unequal pay, banks and finance providers undervalue women's borrowing capacity through presuming an inability to meet loan payments. Seeking business finance compounds the problem.[13]

Yet through the 1980s, wives were regularly tied-in to husbands' loans and finance agreements. Contrasting starkly with women denied finance without a guarantor, the rationale for lending to men with wives as guarantor or cosignatory was that women were deemed conscientious debtors. If a man absconded, lost his job or refused to pay, his wife was easily persuaded to make regular repayments, even if at a lower rate. Women were vulnerable to husbands and partners' persuasion, and intimidated by bank practices prompting a belief that they had no choice but to sign documents. Often, documents were given to men for their wives' signature. Unsurprisingly, this pro-forma approach led some women to believe their signatures were pro-forma, too. Yet contract law asserts 'caveat emptor' – 'let the buyer beware': the law assumes those entering into agreements to buy or borrow know their legal obligations, signing documents in full awareness of their rights and liabilities. Signing under duress or coercion, fraud, mistake or misrepresentation, means equitable remedies apply – but the person asserting these defences must prove them.

In the 20th century, relying on British authority, the Australian High Court endorsed an equitable principle that women's readiness to sign and a husband's capacity to persuade her to do so were influenced by marital status. In *Yerkey v. Jones* [1939] the court recognised marriage exposed wives to financial manipulation or exploitation. Changes, real and perceived, in marriage, relationships and women's role and status meant this subsequently created controversy.[14]

Mr Jones, a man of little means, negotiated a property purchase from Mrs and Mr Yerkey. Mrs Jones owned a house at Walkerville. Enthusiastic about buying the Yerkeys' Payneham property – where besides working the established poultry farm he intended breeding dogs – Jones asked his wife to help. Reluctantly she cosigned the mortgage. In argument with her Jones was persuasive, in execution he was not. The poultry farm failed, the property deteriorated, dog breeding was non-existent. After a year, without advising the Yerkeys, Jones abandoned both his plan and the land. The only payment – £7.10s – came via Mrs Jones' resources: the Yerkeys occupied her Walkerville house temporarily, with

DOI: 10.1057/9781137562357.0007

rental payments credited towards the £3,500 owing on the Payneham land. When the Yerkeys instituted legal action fourteen months after she signed the mortgage, relying upon misrepresentation, mutual and unilateral mistake, and undue influence, Mrs Jones contended she had not understood the transaction.

When making the agreement, although the couples met, Jones led the discussions. Mrs Jones indicated nothing to the Yerkeys of her reluctance about the Payneham property purchase, nor any objection to her husband's plan. Jones fetched the documents from the Yerkeys' solicitors, taking them to his wife and explaining to her that if she did not sign, he would 'be in trouble': he had made written undertakings that her Walkerville property would be mortgaged to part-cover the purchase price. When she signed at the Yerkeys' solicitors' office, Mrs Jones knew her property was at risk of foreclosure and sale to honour the Payneham poultry farm purchase price, if mortgage payments went unpaid.

Mrs Jones' evidence was that she could recollect nothing of what occurred at the solicitors' office, that she was told nothing and did not know she could be liable personally for the £1000 charged against her Walkerville house. The Yerkeys' solicitor did remember, so his evidence prevailed. He said he had explained fully, including Mrs Jones' mortgage liability – she was equally liable with Jones – and as surety for Mr Jones' debt. The surety clause, the solicitor said, was necessary under 'a guarantee mortgage', meaning the Yerkeys as mortgagees could sue Jones, Mrs Jones or both. The clause was 'standard' where a wife 'joins with her husband in mortgaging the wife's estate'. This meant Mrs Jones was both guarantor and a principal in her husband's borrowings. Even if he were released from his obligations, she remained liable.

In *Yerkey v. Jones* on appeal, Rich, J. considered Jones may have been prompted by more than 'his own foolishness', acting with 'less consideration' for Mrs Jones' interests 'than chivalry, not to say propriety, demanded'. Jones may have wished to 'create a situation [causing Mrs Jones] some feeling of reluctance or even of embarrassment' in refusing him. But this did not mean she was deceived about the agreement's nature and purpose, nor that her consent was unreal.

Latham, CJ said that as between 'ordinary' adult persons 'there would be little room' for a defence to an action brought on a document signed in the present circumstances. There was no basis for any of the standard equitable grounds Mrs Jones relied upon: the solicitor explained as required; Jones, whilst 'an optimist as to his prospects of success as a poultry-farmer, ... told her no lies and did not mislead her in any way'. Neither he nor she was under any misapprehension about the terms. That the solicitor was acting for the Yerkeys was clear to Mrs Jones. There was no mistake on the facts. Hence, Mrs Jones' case 'must depend upon some special rules applying to a wife who becomes a surety for her husband'.

Dixon, J. set out that 'special' husband-wife rule:

> ... if a married woman's consent to become a surety for her husband's debt is procured by [him] and without understanding its effect in essential respects she executes an instrument of suretyship which the creditor accepts without dealing directly with her personally, she has a prima-facie right to have it set aside.[15]

It did not save Mrs Jones.

The High Court agreed unanimously that, she being fully informed and aware of all relevant legal matters pertaining to the transaction, and dealing directly through the Yerkeys' solicitors, Mrs Jones was liable for Jones' debt. Even had her husband procured her consent or signature, she remained liable because the Yerkeys had, through their lawyer, provided her with a satisfactory explanation of her liability.

However, Dixon's 'special' husband-wife rule remained intact until contested in the last years of the 20th century. Jurisprudential debate in the UK, North America, Australia and Aotearoa/New Zealand was contradictory.[16] One judicial camp said husbands or male partners, and same sex partners, should enjoy an extension to them of the rule that a wife's 'special' position as 'secondary' to a 'sovereign' husband modifies her responsibility where she is made a surety or guarantor of her husband's debt. The other contended that, women now having equal rights, the 'special' rule considered wives subservient to husbands and should be abolished. Neither approach recognised the historical reality of marriage-as-institution, whereby wives were classed in law differently from husbands, and changing or 'undoing' the law did not automatically mean that socio-cultural assumptions and pressures automatically changed too.

Lord Browne-Wilkinson in *Barclays Bank Plc v. O'Brien & Anor* [1993] was most alert to the dilemma, namely that formal equality differs from substantive equality and saying women have equal rights in law with men, or wives have equal rights in law with husbands, does not make it so. The tension between women's desire to be equal in rights, respect and responsibility, and

DOI: 10.1057/9781137562357.0007

the reality that 'we are not there yet' remains unresolved.[17] This is crucial to gaining a remedy and Magna Carta's demand for access to law: no one will be 'refused right or justice'. Formal equality gained, but substantive equality lacking, what is 'right' and what is 'justice'?

Are wives and husbands equal?

In *Louth v. Diprose* [1992], the Australian High Court held that men's vulnerability can be equal to women's in personal relationships involving money. Mr Diprose and Ms Louth met when living in Tasmania. Louth moved to South Australia. Diprose followed. Predating the interstate move, Louth rejected Diprose's marriage proposal, albeit accepting gifts, payment of utility bills and other gratuities then and later. Diprose, a twice-divorced solicitor, was so 'infatuated' with Louth that he accepted her story that if evicted from her brother's house, where she was then living, she would 'commit suicide'. She said her brother intended selling the house. To save her from eviction, Diprose bought the house in Louth's name. Upon becoming estranged, Diprose asked Louth to transfer the house to him. She refused. He took legal action. By majority, the High Court upheld his claim.

What existed between Louth and Diprose could hardly be equated with affianced persons, much less marriage (legal or de facto). Yet relying on *Page v. Horne* (1848), Brennan, J. considered the relationship analogous to one between a man and his fianceé, where in *Page v. Horne* (1848) she provided a substantial gift to him. Brennan equated the position of a man as equivalent not only to a woman, but an engaged woman – and one back at the time of jurist Blackstone's (1765) state of coverture: 'husbands and wives are one, that one the husband'.

In setting aside the gift in *Page v. Horne*, Lord Langdale, MR observed: '… no one can say what may be the extent of the influence of a man over a woman, whose consent to marriage he has obtained'. Dixon, J. had already taken *Page v. Horne* into account in *Yerkey v. Jones* [1939]. Unlike Brennan, however, Dixon noted the 'distinction drawn between large gifts taken by a man from a woman to whom he is affianced, … and similar gifts by a husband to a wife to which [the presumption of undue influence] does not apply …'. Ignoring Dixon's warning, Brennan reduced *Page v. Horne* to generic 'relationships' and 'emotions', equating Diprose with *Page v. Horne*'s hapless fianceé. For him, Diprose was just as disadvantaged.[18]

DOI: 10.1057/9781137562357.0007

Decided in 1848 – pre-Marriage Women's Property Acts – *Page v. Horne* provides a poor precedent for Brennan's asserted principle. Indeed, it is no precedent. This throws into sharp relief the very problem judges in Brennan's camp do not want to recognise or simply cannot do so.

Individual instances of men overwhelmed by persuasiveness of or pressure from a woman exist. Yet equating Diprose with a woman in coverture is nonsense. Matching his position with a 'wife' ignores entirely the institutional history of marriage and husband-wife relationships as if these lack relevance or impact, or are 'even stevens' as between women and men. It dismisses hundreds of years of history of marriage premised legally, socially and culturally on the proposition 'man the head, woman the subject' (or object). It obscures the position of women who, once engaged, had no independent power over their property and, when married, didn't even own the income they earned. Laws governing women as prospective brides and putative wives never governed men. At the time of *Page v. Horne*, no man was ever in the legal position of a wife. Inferring men now are – through their emotions – is ill-conceived.

Whatever part they might play, this is not simply an issue of 'emotions'.

After *Louth v. Diprose* came *Garcia v. National Australia Bank Ltd* [1998] again addressing the 'special' *Yerkey v. Jones* [1939] husband-wife proposition. *Garcia* saw *Yerkey v. Jones* as setting out two separate circumstances: one where the wife (or partner) knows fully the nature of the transaction when signing documents, but husband (or partner)'s undue influence 'requires' she sign; the other, where the wife (or partner) does not know the transaction's nature yet signs. In the latter, the question is 'does an onus lie on the finance provider?' If, failing to alert or advise her she should seek independent legal advice (for example), the wife (or partner) signs, is she relieved of liability? In *Garcia*, this was framed not in terms of 'emotions' but 'trust and confidence' at the heart of a marriage relationship or one like it. The nature of the transaction not being explained to her properly if at all, Mrs Garcia won relief from the consequences of documents representing her as guarantor of Garcia's gold-dealing transactions.[19]

In *Barclays Bank Plc v. O'Brien & Anor* [1993], the House of Lords unanimously relieved Mrs O'Brien of liability under a surety for her husband's overdraft, a debt to Barclays Bank. She signed documents at a bank branch. Despite instructions from another branch manager, the officer overseeing the transaction did not explain its nature nor advise Mrs O'Brien to

DOI: 10.1057/9781137562357.0007

seek independent legal advice. Thus, where a finance provider knows the person signing a guarantee or similar obligation is wife (or perhaps intimate partner) of the principal borrower, the transaction can be set aside if the husband acts as agent for the finance provider in procuring the wife's signature; or the finance provider has notice of the wife's position vis-à-vis her husband, namely that potentially she is subject to undue influence or misrepresentation. Without a clear explanation to her in her husband's absence, or advice she should seek legal advice independent of her husband, the transaction committing the wife to liability for her husband's debts falls away.[20]

In *Garcia v. National Australia Bank* [1998], Kirby, J. alluded to the past position of wives under Blackstone's (1765) coverture rule – 'husband and wife are one'. Dismissing this as irrelevant, he cited Oliver Wendell Holmes' *Collected Legal Papers*, saying it is 'revolting' to endorse 'no better reason for a rule of law' than its being set 'in the time of Henry IV'. Further, it is 'still more revolting' if the basis for its existence has 'vanished long since,... the rule simply persist[ing] from blind imitation of the past'.[21] But this is not the foundation of contentions that acknowledging the historical subjugation of women is relevant to developing, framing and applying present laws.

No women want laws that constricted women in Magna Carta's time applied today. No plea is made for 'right or justice' to treat women as subordinates of the past. Nor in the name of 'right or justice' do women want paternalistic treatment from the law as if women are of delicate mien requiring 'chivalry' or 'propriety' in Rich's words, or 'classing all women as if in need of special protection' as Kirby admonishes.[22] Women have an obligation to take themselves seriously, recognise their legal responsibilities, and understand they and their signatures count. Yet the law can be framed and applied justly only if a backdrop of historical reality is recognised, the systemic nature of discrimination against women understood. Access to law and remedies to wrongs require it. The past does not cease to exist, simply because judges say so.

Women, rights and (no?) remedy

Yet Brennan and Kirby are not alone – Brennan failing to recognise that women's historical subjugation doesn't apply to men, Kirby considering that in adverting to historical reality, women want 'special favours'.

DOI: 10.1057/9781137562357.0007

Judges must accept women's demand for access to the courts *and* to a remedy, which Magna Carta barons wanted for themselves. The UK Fawcett Society pursued just this, in challenging the Conservative-Liberal Democrat coalition government's austerity measures imposed through the 2010 Budget. Savage cuts ignored Keynesian economics, Thomas Piketty's *Capital*, and Harriet Martineau's 1832–1834 emphasis in *Illustrations of Political Economy* that economics must have human beings at its centre.

Maintaining the 2010 Budget adversely affected women, Fawcett sought judicial review to quash it 'in its entirety'. Beatson, J. refused Fawcett's application. Next seeking declarations that Treasury, HMRC and the Chancellor had, through the budget, failed to comply with their general Sex Discrimination Act 1975 duty to have 'due regard' to eliminating unlawful discrimination and harassment, and promote equality of opportunity between women and men, in *R. (On the Application of the Fawcett Society) v. Chancellor of the Exchequer* [2010], Fawcett went before Ouseley, J. contending the government ought to have conducted and published a Budget 'Gender Equality Impact Assessment' (GEIA).[23]

Fawcett attacked the complete budget and the budget's 'spending envelope', namely departmental limits governing conduct of their comprehensive spending review. At the outset, Ouseley conceded Fawcett's counsel made 'some important and interesting arguments' – legal teams will have recognised the phrase as immediately presaging that the application was lost, as indeed it was. Ouseley next observed, rightly so, that political disagreements about the budget – public expenditure cuts, their nature, tax increases and their nature, job cuts and pay freezes – were not for the court. He must follow the Statutory Code of Guidance to public authorities, which says 'due regard' is a matter for the court, weight given to promoting gender equality being 'proportionate to its relevance to a particular function'.[24]

No GEIA had been produced, but the government's counsel submitted and Ouseley agreed that the government was entitled to address any impact of budget provisions on gender equality objectives by reference to specific individual items, not the overall budget. Fawcett contested this, saying it enabled the budget's 'cumulative impact' on equality of opportunity 'to be ignored', with 'swings and roundabouts' also 'falling out of the picture'. Ouseley nonetheless accepted the 'polycentric nature of the decision-making process', necessarily relying on assumptions, leading to 'questionable utility...of any results' of a GEIA attempt. Anyway, 'no

DOI: 10.1057/9781137562357.0007

other government [had] produced such an assessment for a previous Budget'. Further, it was perfectly legal for a government to address gender equality impact of the budget line by line, for the cumulative effect and 'swings and roundabouts' could be identified thus. That this had not, in any event, been done, Ouseley ignored.

As to the public spending envelope, Fawcett submitted:

▸ as it was 'not possible to challenge limits set when the precise distribution of funds within departmental Budgets comes to be dealt with'; and
▸ if 'that limitation means that an otherwise remedial gender inequality exists', then the government took 'at least an arguably unlawful approach'.

Ouseley could not see it. Anyway, he accepted, 'no door ... is irretrievably closed'. Departmental budgets 'have considerable scope for reallocation of monies ...' whereby 'otherwise irremediable gender inequality' could be addressed – 'if it arises'. In any event, 'high level economic judgements' are required as to 'when and how best' to address gender equality requirements.

Whether such 'high-level economic judgements' were actually made is unclear, although several areas were proposed and apparently accepted by Fawcett as having been subjected to a GIEA. The government extended various mea culpas for GIEA's not done, or done too late. For Ouseley, these provided no basis for the declarations Fawcett sought. The matter was now 'academic', he said, and, anyway, the erring government departments would carry out the impact assessment in any event.

As to disputes between the parties on whether potential gender bias should be considered from the outset, or policy formulated then considered for gender bias, Fawcett lost. Similarly with government contentions that some matters clearly lacked any gender impact. On the one hand, Ouseley said it was 'perfectly sensible' to wait until policy 'has been adequately formulated' to provide 'a clear basis upon which its gender equality impact can be assessed'.[25] On the other, although it was evident that an assessment on a household basis (as opposed to one disaggregating data exposing single parent households and the sex/gender of household heads) would affect assessment of benefit cuts as impacting more on women than men, this was accepted as 'a perfectly reasonable argument'. Nonetheless, it required a 'rational assessment' by the relevant department 'given the nature of the task and ... high level of specialist

DOI: 10.1057/9781137562357.0007

knowledge' possessed. (The court hastily added that 'those who oppose them' – embodied in the Fawcett Society – possessed such specialist knowledge, too.) In any event, such opposing viewpoints provided no basis for saying the government was acting unlawfully: 'I am satisfied there has been no breach ... of the duty to have regard to the objectives of promoting equality of opportunity between genders'.

Ultimately delay affected the decision. Judicial review must be brought promptly. Here, initial proceedings began five weeks after the budget announcement. Delays meant, however, that budget implementation was well advanced and the impact of interruption was 'incalculable', including that on the country's relations with Europe and globally.

Yet it is difficult to leave the *Fawcett Case* with other than a sinking heart. Naughty school girls in the courtroom? Leave it to the big boys, girlies?[26] All Lord Neaves' fears come to roost, with women not only in universities and trained as lawyers, but appearing authoritatively in court? What next? More women on the bench?

That women persist in seeking justice through law confirms their belief that some courts, some judges may recognise systemic discrimination – not only outside the courtroom, but within it. Some courts, some judges may acknowledge the power of the past. Some courts, some judges may comprehend that hundreds of years of women's activism before and after Magna Carta have, when contesting the institutionalised patriarchy Wollstonecraft critiqued in 1792 and Pizan satirised in 1604, gone far without yet securing both formal and substantive equality with men.

Courts have a responsibility to entertain women's just claims, applying Magna Carta in its call: 'To no one will we sell, to no one will we refuse or delay, right or justice.' Justice must incorporate women's meanings. Sometimes, women do win. Yet still, women wait.

Notes

1   *Fares v. Box Hill College of TAFE* (1992), illustrating intersectionality in law and legal process.
2   *Leves v. Haines* (1986); Scutt, 'Achieving the "impossible"' in Scutt, *Sexual Gerrymander*, 1994, p. 228; Editorial, 'Melinda Leves', 1986.
3   Holt, *Magna Carta*, 2015, p. 262.
4   Holt, *Magna Carta* 2015, p. 46; Beloff, 'Magna Carta', 2015, p. 6.
5   Wollstonecraft, *A Vindication*, 1792, 1999, p. 96.

DOI: 10.1057/9781137562357.0007

6   Kempe, *The Book*, 1438, 2000, 2004.

7   Chancery rules protected married women's equitable interests – see *Grigby v. Cox* (1750); *Pybus v. Smith* (1790); *Yerkey v. Jones* [1939] at 10–12; also *Bank of Victoria Ltd v. Mueller* (1925).

8   Staves, *Married Women's Separate Property*, 1990.

9   Scutt, 'Cash or Kind', 1997.

10   Kempe, *The Book*, 1438, 2004, p. 2.

11   See Kanowitz, *Women and the Law*, 1969, p. 39; Donovan, 'Retreat from Yerkey v. Jones', 1996.

12   Lemire, *Business of Everyday Life*, 2005, pp. 41–42.

13   See Hill, '5 times it's more expensive', 2015; Anti-Discrimination Board, NSW, *Report*, 1987; DeCrow, *Sexist Justice*, 1975, pp. 125–156; following research comes from these sources and Scutt, 'Cash or Kind', 1997, p. 149.

14   *Yerkey v. Jones* [1939]. UK: cases cited therein and *Barclays Bank plc v. O'Brien (AP)* [1993] (see later); US: Texas case *US v. Yazell*, 1966; also Donovan, 'Retreat from Yerkey v. Jones' (1996).

15   *Yerkey v. Jones* [1939], at 16.

16   See *Garcia v. National Australia Bank Ltd* [1998]; *Day v. Shaw and Shaw* [2014]; *Wilkinson v. ASB Bank Ltd* [1998], adopting *Barclays Bank Plc v. O'Brien* [1993]. On Canadian sureties, Cipollone, 'The Liabilities of Securities', 2014.

17   *Barclays Bank Plc v. O'Brien & Anor* [1993]. Browne-Wilkinson emphasised same sex partners' rights, fellow judges unanimously agreeing.

18   *Page v. Horne* (1848), at 807; *Yerkey v. Jones* [1939], at 675; *Louth v. Diprose* [1992], at 6.

19   *Garcia v. National Australia Bank Ltd* [1998], at 21, 30. In *Garcia* Kirby, J. adopted *Barclays Bank*.

20   *Barclays Bank* [1993], at 11–13ff.

21   Holmes, 'The Path', 1897, 1920, 1952; cited Kirby, *Garcia v. National Australia Bank Ltd* [1998], at 18.

22   *Garcia v. National Australia Bank* [1998], at 19.

23   Sex Discrimination Act 1975, s. 76A; Sex Discrimination Act 1975 (Public Authorities)(Statutory Duties) Order 2006, art. 2 – preparation and publication of gender equality schemes.

24   *R. (On the Application of the Fawcett Society) v. Chancellor of the Exchequer* [2010], at 4; following quotations 6–7, 8–9, 12, and 13–16.

25   *Fawcett Society v. Chancellor of the Ex1ochequer* [2010], at 16; following quotations at 16.

26   In 1990s Australia, a judge told a female solicitor to 'sit down girlie' – which became the title of a regular satirical *Alternative Law Journal* (*Legal Service Bulletin*) column.

DOI: 10.1057/9781137562357.0007

6

No Taxation without Representation

Abstract: *Magna Carta barons wanted representation and rights to fairer taxes. Women want the same. Scutt traverses US, UK, Canadian, Aotearoa/New Zealand and Australian women's campaigns for voting rights and fair taxation based on equal pay. Australia's Vida Goldstein, Canada's Nellie McClung, in the US Susan B. Anthony and Elizabeth Cady Stanton, the UK's Barbara Bodichon, Emily Wilding Davison, Dora Montefiore, Annie Kenney and the Pankhursts campaigned for women's rights. Some voting rights campaigners were prosecuted and tortured by forced-feeding. Some refused to be counted in the 1911 Census. Some refused to pay taxes. Spurred on by injustice, US women of Pawtucket mills, Aotearoa/New Zealand's Harriet Morison, Canadians, Australians and British women campaigned for industrial rights and equal pay – this a just cause not yet won.*

Keywords: equal pay campaigns; women and 1911 Census; women and equal pay; women and the vote; women's campaign against taxation; women's taxation rights; women's vote campaign; women's voting rights

Scutt, Jocelynne A. *Women and Magna Carta: A Treaty for Rights or Wrongs?* Basingstoke: Palgrave Macmillan, 2016. DOI: 10.1057/9781137562357.0008.

 DOI: 10.1057/9781137562357.0008

> No scutage nor aid shall be imposed on our kingdom, unless by common counsel of our kingdom...
>
> *Magna Carta, cap. 12*

Taxation and Magna Carta

On 2 April 1911, Emily Wilding Davison hid in a cupboard in the Chapel of St Mary Undercroft in the House of Commons. It was Census night. Her form was completed, her family name appearing as 'Davidson'. Clearly, she did not write it. The space for her postal address says: 'Found hiding in crypt of Westminster Hall.' A pencilled note on the bottom left-hand corner advises '3/4/11 Since Saturday'.[1]

Why was Davison there? Who found her? What, 'since Saturday', did she eat and drink?

Resistance to government demands has a long history, as does the assertion that government has a right to make demands only through the people's collective consent. Predating Davison by almost 900 years and Magna Carta by at least 150 years, the legendary Lady Godiva's ride is recounted in Ranulf Higden's (c.1280–1364) *Polychronicon* and by Roger of Wendover (d. 1236) in his *Chronicles*. Protesting at heavy taxes imposed on Coventry's citizens by her husband, Leofric, Earl of Mercer, Godiva won them a reprieve by accepting her husband's challenge to parade naked on horseback through the streets.[2]

The cry 'no taxation without representation' resounds from Magna Carta down the centuries. The campaign for US independence from King George III and his government, when rebels used Magna Carta to win freedom from a colonial master, is not unique. Women consistently objected, for women in the colonies and under the colonial master were denied the vote, equal pay and access to equally paying trades, professions and public office, yet were taxed. Wives suffered the indignity of being denied property and income ownership rights, while bearing the inequities heaped upon their single sisters. Their income was owned by their husbands, and taxed, too. Whether there was joint taxation or individual taxation, earned income and property were calculated 'in' to revenue and women's earnings were subject to tax laws, without representation.

DOI: 10.1057/9781137562357.0008

In their struggle for women's right to vote and stand for and sit in parliament, women refused to be counted in the 1911 census. Some refused to pay taxes, too. How many defied the census count is unknown, although estimates set it at 'several thousand'. Many may have been counted, though on strike. Ironically, a determined Davison was recorded twice: 'resident' when hiding in the below-stairs cupboard and at her Russell Square residential address. Who completed that return is also unclear.[3]

Taxation was central to Magna Carta, money the signatories' major concern. Taxation appears in various forms, particularly in caps 2 through 14. Cap. 14, like cap. 12, refers to scutages and aids, the former paid by tenants-in-chief instead of providing military service to the king, the latter 'payments owed by the tenant-in-chief to the king as part of…tenurial obligations' and 'general taxes paid by everyone in the realm'. Women were not exempt.

Reflecting upon the lead-up to Magna Carta, in *King John* Stephen Church observes that widespread refusal to pay taxes due at Michaelmas 1214, after sixty years' compliance, provoked a 'startling moment' in Exchequer history. The summer before Magna Carta saw 'serious and sustained resistance'. Following this lead, freedom from taxation without representation was paramount for America's colonial agitators seeking freedom from British rule and King George III's tyranny. They claimed Magna Carta as the foundation for the US Constitution.[4]

Herein lies a paradox. Whilst Magna Carta proclaimed 'no taxation without representation', taxes to be paid only by consent, given collectively, women as part of that community were ignored. The US Constitution similarly ignored women as part of the community entitled to consent and representation.

No representation, no taxation!

On the morning of 20 July 1848 at Seneca Falls, Elizabeth Cady Stanton read the women's Declaration of Independence. Framed on the US Declaration of Independence, made less than a century earlier, the women's Declaration began:

> When, in the course of human events, it becomes necessary for one portion of the family of man to assume among the people of the earth a position different from that which they have hitherto occupied…a decent respect to

DOI: 10.1057/9781137562357.0008

the opinions of mankind requires that they should declare the causes that impel them to such a course ...[5]

A history of men's treatment of women was condemned as having as its direct aim 'the establishment of an absolute tyranny ...' Substantiating this, the Declaration said, were facts denoting women's status, including 'depriving her of all rights as a married woman' then:

> [I]f single and the owner of property, he has taxed her to support a government which recognizes her only when her property can be made profitable to it.

Like Magna Carta and the US Declaration of Independence, the Seneca Falls Declaration links imposition of taxes to lack of representation:

> He has never permitted her to exercise her inalienable right to the elective franchise.
>
> He has compelled her to submit to laws, in the formation of which she had no voice.
>
> ...
>
> Having deprived her of this first right of a citizen, the elective franchise, thereby leaving her without representation in the halls of legislation, he has oppressed her on all sides.

Fifty years on, across the Atlantic the Women's Tax Resistance League flew the banner of tax resistance. Founding members Louisa Garrett Anderson, Cicely Hamilton of *Marriage as a Trade* (1909) fame, Edith How-Martyn, Margaret Nevinson, Anne Cobden Sanderson, Sime Seruya, Maud Arncliffe Sennett, Lena Ashwell, Minnie Turner, Beatrice Harraden, Evelyn Sharp, Eveline Haverfield, Margory Lees and Dora (Fuller) Montefiore refused to pay tax, and were punished. They were not alone. A link with Magna Carta was established when Mrs Emmeline Pethick-Lawrence visited the John Hampden monument at Chalgrove, celebrating the Buckinghamshire MP for Aylesbury who had refused to pay King Charles I's Ship Money. Buckingham featured in Magna Carta history directly, too, for knights Robert and Henry of Braybrook, father and son and sheriffs of Northamptonshire and Bedfordshire-Buckinghamshire, raised large sums for John's Exchequer, prompting barons' ire.[6]

Earlier Montefiore, returning in 1891 to Britain from Australia (where, from 1874, she established the New South Wales Womanhood Suffrage League), adopted her 'no taxation' stand during the Boer War 'in the making of which [she] had no voice'. In 1904 and 1905, sheriffs confiscated

DOI: 10.1057/9781137562357.0008

goods to the value of moneys she was said to owe. A year later, backed by the WSPU's Theresa Billington and Annie Kenney, Montefiore barricaded herself and her maid, 'a keen suffragist', into her Hammersmith house for six weeks. Women demonstrated outside, WSPU members spoke from the house steps, and Montefiore declaimed from an upstairs window. The postman delivered daily 'encouraging... [though] a few sadly vulgar and revolting... budgets of correspondence' and the weekly wash arrived '... over the high garden wall'. Milk and bread were delivered by loyal neighbourhood tradespeople. Lancashire lads offered the 'besieged women' support. Members of Parliament wrote, describing it as 'the most logical demonstration'. The small rear garden provided the women with fresh air and a journalist delivered a loaf of bread over the wall to 'The Fort', asking Kenney to hand it up whilst photographers captured the moment. A police officer remained throughout the entire 'siege' – broken only when bailiffs entered, traversing a stoop above which a banner cried: 'Women should vote for the laws they obey and the taxes they pay'. Twenty-two police attended the auction of Montefiore's goods at rooms in Hammersmith, where she, her colleagues and sympathisers stood by, determined not to engage in violence despite the injustice.[7]

Another tax resister (and census evader), Miss Clara Lee of Thistledown, Letchworth, wrote to *The Vote* telling how she forced Inland Revenue Authorities to acknowledge two errors in a demand for Inhabited House Duty of 8s. 9d. One, she said, 'ought not to have occurred seeing we have had compulsory education since 1868'. In the other, Inland Revenue categorised her as a 'nurseries and market gardens' tax payer. The 'nearest connection' she had to either 'was that under the Lloyd George Insurance Act [she] was classed with agricultural labourers'. GR Simpson, Inland Revenue – Surveyor of Taxes, responded to her protest:

> Madam, – Referring to your letter of the 9th inst., I much regret that £1.1s.9d. was included upon your demand note in error – the entry relating to the next person upon the collector's return. – Yours faithfully...[8]

Lee's letter to *The Vote* admonished:

> Is this the exactness of the work for which women, as well as men, pay so heavily? How long would a commercial firm exist, if it allowed such errors? How long would the public tolerate such mistakes by women workers...? The title of idiot, lunatic and criminal must revert to the people responsible for such a condition of things. The 8s. 9d. Inhabited House Duty has now

DOI: 10.1057/9781137562357.0008

been deducted from my claim of return Income tax; this seems an unusual proceeding...

Married women did not escape. As Hilary Frances recounts in *The Women's Suffrage Movement*, Charlotte Despard's long-time companion, Mrs Kate Harvey, 'barricaded her home against bailiffs, withstanding an eight month siege'. Refusing to pay her gardener's National Insurance contributions, she was imprisoned for two months. The attempted sale of Harvey's goods was prohibited by chaos created by women demonstrating, incurring the tax collector losses of £7.0s.0d.[9]

Under joint income tax provisions husbands ostensibly paid their wives' income tax, receiving any refunds or abatements. As married women generally paid the tax, this was another injustice. Frances reports Dr Elizabeth Wilks' tactics. Initially, Dr Wilks paid the tax. Initially, Wilks paid the tax. Then, joining the Women's Tax Resistance League, she 'fully exploited' tax anomalies. Noting her husband's receiving and often retaining the abatement, she refused to pay. Her confiscated property was returned, because joint tax provisions did not require her to pay. The Revenue Office took action against her husband, Mark Wilks. When Dr Wilks refused to divulge her income to him, the Revenue Office presented Wilks with an estimate. Earning a teacher's far lower income, he could not meet the bill. He was committed to Brixton Prison. Speeches were made in the House of Lords, Wilks was released after two weeks, and the tax was never paid.

Another husband, resident in Aotearoa/New Zealand, caused ineffable grief to both Revenue Office and legal system. Frances reports that first the one, then the other, was tied up for months addressing unpaid taxes of Dr Burns, his wife.

In *Australian Woman Suffrage*, Audrey Oldfield notes married women (like single women) were liable for land tax, at least from 1898. 'As far as we know,' she says, 'no Australian woman refused to pay her tax ...' But whether or not alluding to Magna Carta, women did protest. In *The Dawn* campaign, Louisa Lawson published a pro forma letter to go to revenue collectors: 'I pay this tax under strong protest, because I have no vote.' Winning the vote in 1894, women in South Australia did not take this stand.[10] So, too, women in Aotearoa/New Zealand, from 1893 being enfranchised, *Votes for Women* by Atkinson observing:

> On 19 September 1893, when the governor, Lord Glasgow, signed a new Electoral Act..., New Zealand became the first self-governing country in

DOI: 10.1057/9781137562357.0008

the world to grant the right to vote to all adult women...[A] truly radical change...[11]

Campaigning to vote

Two years before the Paris Commune recognised women's voting rights, on 10 December 1869 Wyoming was the first US legislature to extend suffrage to women.[12] The struggle continued elsewhere, antipodean women actively campaigning for voting rights meeting resistance as did their sisters in Canada, the UK and the US. Just as John Stuart Mill promoted women's voting rights at Westminster, some members of other legislatures acknowledged the injustice, introducing private members' bills.

The year Wyoming women became voters, British judges in *Chorlton v. Lings* (1868–1869) used the Great Reform Act of 1832 to deprive thousands of registered voters of their voting rights simply because they were women. Sixty years earlier, at Mary Smith's behest, in 1832, Henry Hunt MP presented the first House of Commons 'votes for women' petition. In 1866, Mill tabled Barbara Bodichon's 1500-signature petition, organised through the Women's Suffrage Committee. When the Second Reform Act 1867 was introduced, Mill proposed an amendment incorporating votes for all householders, regardless of sex. Although unsuccessful, thenceforth Bills proposing women's enfranchisement came before the Commons almost annually.[13]

In Victoria, sixty years after Smith's petition and thirty years after Bodichon's, Vida Goldstein (1869–1949) led women in compiling the 260m long, 200mm wide 'Monster Petition'. Presented by the premier – whose wife Jane Munro signed as 'Mrs James Munro' – the Women's Suffrage Petition proclaimed 'Women should Vote on Equal terms with Men'. The year? 1891. How many signed? Some 30,000. The outcome? No votes for women.[14]

Despite a myth that Australian women won the vote without struggle, campaigning women were disparaged, vilified and derided – often by politicians and 'respectable' men, including judges. The *Bulletin* published vile and often vicious 'cartoons'. Henrietta Dugdale (1827–1918) in particular was lampooned: 'I wouldn't want to be at the ballot box beside such a mustachioed woman', said one politician.[15] Nonetheless, after South Australian women were enfranchised, women of Western

DOI: 10.1057/9781137562357.0008

Australia won in 1899, with Victoria the last state, in 1908. Women gained the vote nationally in 1902, however racism denied Indigenous Australian women (apart from South Australia) voting rights until some fifty years later, state-by-state.

An MP's desire to scupper the 1894 enfranchisement Bill entirely by an amendment enabling women to stand for Parliament meant South Australian women won that right. Federally, women won the right to stand, the first country in the world granting both rights. Goldstein was the first woman in the British Empire registering to run: she, with Nellie Martell (1855–1940) and Mary Anne Moore Bentley (1865–1953) stood for the Senate in 1903, and Selina Siggins (1878–1964) for the House of Representatives. None was elected, however Goldstein, campaigning distinctively with Magic Lantern technology, won thousands of votes and stood thrice more. Lecturing in the US in 1902, the Australian Electoral Act having won international attention, Goldstein was acknowledged by President Theodore Roosevelt demanding to meet the only woman in the country entitled to vote in national elections.[16]

Global interaction was common. From the antipodes women travelled to Britain, Europe, Eastern Europe, the Pacific and the Americas, lecturing and exchanging tactics and ideas. In 1908, artist Dora Meeson Coates (1869–1955) created the 'Trust the Women' banner commemorating Australian women's enfranchisement. Australian women carried it in the 1908 and 1911 London women's suffrage processions. Headed 'Commonwealth of Australia', recognising Australia's link with the 'mother of Parliaments', the banner read: 'Trust the Women, Mother, as I have done'.[17] Voting had not driven Australian women mad, debased the elective process, nor undermined democracy. With positive consequences in Australia, why not the UK?

The Australian prime minister's wife, Margaret Fisher, marched in London in 1911, alongside Goldstein, Emily McGowen, Lady Cockburn (wife of South Australia's premier) and Lady Stout (wife of a former Aotearoa/New Zealand prime minister).[18] Fisher's husband introduced maternity allowances and recognised the necessity for women's political equality. Yet the majority of British politicians remained unconvinced. Over time, British women had gained rights of election to school boards, sanitation boards, poor law authorities and other local bodies. This added to their entitlement, decided in *Olive v. Ingram* (1738), to be elected as sextons, although the classification of that post as a private trust fed the prejudice against women's entitlement to enter public office. As Bruley

DOI: 10.1057/9781137562357.0008

notes in *Women in Britain Since 1900*, the local government-Westminster divide remained immutable.[19] Thus demands of Magna Carta barons laying foundations for a democratically elected Parliament remained outside women's status, struggle and station.

British women were arrested, manhandled by police, imprisoned, tortured, and denied political prisoner ranking. Prime minister Herbert Asquith's dismissal of women's claims was relentless. His government initiated then endorsed brutalising women. Notoriously, the Cat and Mouse Act 1913 sanctioned torture, yet the politicians passing it did so without compunction. Styled 'an Act to provide for the temporary discharge of prisoners whose further detention in prison is undesirable on account of the condition of their health', this disgraceful piece of legislation meant women debilitated by the torture of force-feeding were released then, once deemed recovered, returned to captivity, the punishment resumed. That a few voices might be raised in 'nay' to its passage could not counter the UK Parliament's acquiescence to, indeed support of, legislation promoting shamefully wholesale dehumanising of women simply wanting a democratic voice. Ironically, despite his being characterised a 'tyrant', though he starved Matilde De Briouze and her son William to death over a fealty and land dispute, John had not treated Magna Carta's barons at Runnymede in this way.[20]

Commons Conciliation Bills introduced in 1910, 1911 and 1912 proposed votes for women property owners or 'heads of households'. The first two languished in committee, the last was defeated by a small majority (208 'for', 222 'against'), comprising women's suffrage opponents, MPs rejecting a class-voting rights connection, and those jealous of their own political priorities.[21] The 1912 Bill's proposer, Mr Agg-Gardiner, deplored the 'conduct of certain persons who desire to obtain … the enfranchisement of women', regarding them 'as victims of a probably well-intentioned and perhaps earnest but certainly misguided enthusiasm'. Yet equally, he commiserated with the 'countless' disenfranchised women active in public affairs as 'members of town councils, boards of guardians and Royal Commissions', participating on public platforms and being 'prominent members of political associations'. 'Why', he asked, should women holding 'highest distinction in the realms of literature, of science and of art' be denied the vote?[22] Seconder Sir Alfred Mond decried 'setting up woman as a sort of china doll in a sacred hearth to be worshipped from afar', with five million women earning their own living and two million 'engaged in industrial pursuits'. Furthermore:

DOI: 10.1057/9781137562357.0008

To widen the sphere of influence of women is a good thing. It is good for the wife and it is good for the mother, and it is good ... for the home of the citizen, [so] argument against it ought to be abandoned.

Viscount Helmsley, for the 'no-es', maintained the 'whole position and functions of Parliament would be altered ...': the 'two sexes sitting together ... would no doubt alter the whole tone and whole feeling' of Parliament. Men could not discuss and debate freely beside women, whose 'mental equilibrium ... is not as stable as [that] of the male sex ...'. Science proved it. Meanwhile Eugene Watson said that despite his 'aye' in the past, he would now vote 'nay' as 'Suffragists' militancy' meant that 'even in this House' it was impossible to 'meet your wife as you used to' or 'take your American cousin, coming over here, up to the Ladies Gallery ...'. For Harold Baker, the vote was 'a badge not of superiority, but of difference' lying in the 'masculine character and coercive power ... adapted for the governance of alien races and ... safeguarding of our Empire ...'. Perhaps, for him, denying British women votes would somehow safeguard from afar the population of those parts of the Empire that had enfranchised women.

War's outbreak in 1914 established a truce. Emmeline Pankhurst (1858–1928) and Christabel Pankhurst's (1880–1958) followers went into war work. Their capitulation echoed Lord Curzon's words in the 1912 debate:

What is the good of talking about the equality of the sexes? The first whiz of the bullet, the first boom of the cannon and where is the equality of the sexes then?

Sylvia Pankhurst (1882–1960) and her sister Adela Pankhurst (1885–1961) worked for peace. Dismissed by her mother to Australia, Adela joined Goldstein's Women's Peace Army, employing militant tactics to oppose conscription and campaign against bread prices soaring with every wheat shipment to feed British troops.[23]

At war's end, Asquith conceded, was lauded, and women over thirty with property holdings won the vote. Torture and police brutality were ignored. So, for some, were the inequalities inherent in the Representation of the People [sic] Act 1918. All men over twenty-one years, without property qualification, were enfranchised and only 40% of women were: those over thirty with property could vote. The rest waited ten years more for the 1928 Equal Franchise Act.

Women's war work made a difference in North America, too. From at least the 1870s women's organisations orchestrated a Canadian 'votes

DOI: 10.1057/9781137562357.0008

for women' campaign. Emily Stowe's (1831–1903) work with her Toronto Women's Literacy Club colleagues came to fruition through continued work of Nellie McClung's (1873–1951) Manitoba Political Equality League with others, when Winnipeg women won the vote in 1916. Ontario followed, then the Military Voters Act 1917 extended voting rights to nurses and armed service women, followed by the Wartime Election Act 1918 granting votes to women with husbands, sons or fathers serving overseas. Finally women of twenty-one and over gained the vote from 1 January 1919, although Quebec women didn't win provincial voting rights until 1940.[24]

For the US, the First World War began in 1917. Women secured the vote at its end. Passed by Congress on 4 June 1919, the 19th Amendment was ratified on 18 August 1920. Congress having power to enforce it, the Amendment provides:

> The right of citizens of the United States to vote shall not be denied or abridged by the United States or by any State on account of sex.

When in *Hawke v. Smith* (1920) Ohio challenged the 18th (Prohibition) and 19th Amendments under a state provision that 6% of voters could require a referendum on legislative ratification of a federal constitutional amendment, the win wobbled. The Ohio Supreme Court upheld the challenge, jeopardising women's voting rights. However, the US Supreme Court overruled Ohio, declaring the Ohio provision infringed the Constitution. Thenceforth, women had the right to vote. Did this achieve women's Magna Carta claims?

Equal tax, but (un)equal pay?

Like the barons, women at Seneca Falls wanted to end grievances, not just air them. The vote was not enough. Women clamoured not only for Magna Carta's representation rights and consent to taxation. Though not claimed in Magna Carta (unsurprising, in women's absence), equal access to education, training, job opportunities and equal pay were fundamental, and fundamentally linked to taxation:

> He has taken from her all right to property, even to the wages she earns.
>
> He has monopolized nearly all the profitable employments, and from those she is permitted to follow, she receives but a scanty remuneration.

DOI: 10.1057/9781137562357.0008

He closes against her all the avenues to wealth and distinction, which he considers most honorable to himself. As a teacher of theology, medicine, or law, she is not known.

He has denied her the facilities for obtaining a thorough education – all colleges being closed against her.[25]

Across the Atlantic some sixty years later, men at Westminster asserted women's place was not in the industrial world – at least not at the top. In the 1912 Conciliation Bill debate, Viscount Helmsley said that lack of women as business leaders meant not only that they shouldn't be there, but women lacked the capacity:

Where are the women merchants and the women bankers? Where are the women directors of great undertakings... I can imagine very few undertakings in which women exercise an equal share of the control with the men.[26]

Meanwhile, women worked industriously in factories, hospitals, schools, service, shops, offices – all at lower pay than men alongside or doing 'men's jobs', more highly valued and with higher pay. Yet women paid the same property taxes, council, water and utility rates, stamp duty and any other government imposts, receiving no income tax reduction – even if calculated progressively, women paid more for many services. In 1873, in 'The Medical Education of Women', Sophia Jex-Blake observed that women suffered 'indirectly imposed... heavy pecuniary tax', instancing Apothecaries Hall compelling Elizabeth Garrett 'to pay very heavy fees for separate and private tuition' to qualify for medical practice.[27] Forty years on, women continued to bear additional imposts, at all levels. Women's hairdressing, clothing, and laundry were more expensive. It was claimed women were profligate, and proposed they should cut their own hair (or ask a friend), make their own clothes, and do their own washing.[28]

Working-class women, like middle-class and aristocratic women, joined the voting rights struggle. Detractors and opponents existed amongst women of all classes, joining male opponents, sometimes equally vociferously. Division occurred in equal pay campaigns, too – some women arguing the 'rightness' of men earning more than women, whatever women's tax liability or household responsibilities. For some, 'man' equals 'head of household' and held sway, despite many women adopting the role, whether the household had a man or not. Men could be invalids, alcoholics, spendthrifts, gamblers or selfish. Whether or not the

DOI: 10.1057/9781137562357.0008

law made women subordinate to men in child custody or guardianship, women were responsible for children's nurture and care.

When in 1837 Caroline Sheridan Norton wrote *Separation of Mother and Child*, she launched a women's custody rights campaign, because her three children by George Norton, wife beater, 'belonged' to him alone, he being their natural and legal father. Yet without an income, how could women – had they custodial rights – care for children financially, whatever their mothering ability? Without a private income or a job, women could not even support themselves. Women unable to go out to work took in lodgers, washing and ironing, or went into others' homes to work, hoping to live-in despite restricted independence. For women, the cry was not only 'no taxation without representation', but 'no equal tax, without equal pay'.

As men unionised, so did women. Australian women's unions predated men's: established in 1882, the Melbourne Tailoresses Union fought for women's wages, lower hours and industrial safety, going on strike in 1883 when employers refused to answer their log of claims. Demanding and getting a Royal Commission into outwork or piecework, their agitation and organisation prodded the Victorian government into passing the 1884 Factory Act. In Aotearoa/New Zealand women workers organised, too. In 'They will never crush out the Union!' Ciaran Doolin identifies Harriet Morison (1862–1925) – 'influential in the suffragette movement' and leading the Tailoresses' Union – blending industrial with political activism and, in 1889, winning increased wages and improved conditions.[29]

For the UK, in *Women in Britain* Bruley recounts women's prominent role in industrial agitation, alongside general labour dissent, particularly during 1910–1911 in Birmingham. Women chain-makers gained a rise from 4–6s weekly 'to 10–11s for a 55-hour week', to be implemented in six months. However:

> By September of 1910, 700 women chain-makers were refusing to work at the old rate...[Despite being] isolated home workers...spread over a large area,...they received tremendous support from the Anti-Sweating League and many labour movement bodies.[30]

Employers capitulated after ten weeks.

Women's industrial activism occurred in North America, too. The proposition that women were reluctant to make demands of rapacious employers rings hollow against the facts. A Rhode Island strike predated

DOI: 10.1057/9781137562357.0008

the famed 1850s Lowell Mill workers' strike, when in May 1824 mill owners cut wages. Uniting with factory workers, farmers and artisans, 102 women led a strike spreading through the eight Pawtucket mills. With mill doors blocked:

> For a week, the village descended into chaos. Workers and farmers marched *en masse* to the mill owners' houses, hurling rocks and insults [in] the first factory strike in the United States ....[31]

What would Magna Carta barons, so many northerners, have made of this? Is it unrelated that women in England's north figured prominently in working women's activism for fair pay and the franchise struggle? Birmingham union official Julie Varley (1871–1952) and Liverpool organiser Mary Bamber (1874–1938) rose to prominence with the rise of suffragette militancy. Working-class women from Lancashire and Cheshire 'linked suffrage, socialist and labour movement involvement'. In Bruley's words, with networks of local groups, the North of England Suffrage Society, affiliated to the wider suffrage movement, was the north-west centre of suffrage agitation.[32]

In declaring their rights to vote and equal pay so that their wages might be fair, and their taxes too, women affirmed a bill of rights against states exploiting them economically while denying them equality. In proclaiming their own Magna Carta, women trod the footprints of barons who never would have contemplated this consequence of their revolt against a king.

Notes

1 www.parliament.uk, Living Heritage – Women and the Vote.

2 Roger of Wendover: Carpenter, *Magna Carta*, 2015; 'From Dot to Domesday'.

3 www.parliament.uk, Living Heritage – 1911Census.co.uk; Liddington and Crawford, 'Women do not count', 2011.

4 Carpenter, *Magna Carta*, 2015, pp. 16–17; Church, *King John*, 2015, p. 213; US founders relied on Magna Carta 1225, following 1215 provisions.

5 Elizabeth Cady Stanton Papers Project; Gordon (ed.), *Elizabeth Cady Stanton Papers Project*, 1997, vol. 1, chapter 23; following quotations this source.

6 Cartwright, 'No vote, no tax', 2011; Carpenter, *Magna Carta*, 2015, p. 231.

7 Montefiore, *From a Victorian*, 1925, Chapter VI, 'Women Must Vote'

8 Quoted Lee, Letter to Editor, 1912. Lee evaded the census with Mrs Margaret Kineton Parkes (1865–1920), of Flat 10, Talbot House, 98 St Martin's Lane

DOI: 10.1057/9781137562357.0008

(from 1910 Women's Tax Resistance League office); following quotation this source.

9   Frances, 'Pay the Piper!' 2009. Dr Wicks and Dr Burns' exploits appear here.
10 Oldfield, *Australian Woman Suffrage*, 1993.
11 Neill Atkinson, *Votes for Women*, 2002.
12 This Day in History, *Old West – Wyoming*.
13 www.parliament.uk, Living Heritage – Women and the Vote, 'Petitions'.
14 Parliament of Victoria, *Women's Suffrage Petition*.
15 See generally, Brownfoot, 'Dugdale, Henrietta Augusta', 1992.
16 Australian Electoral Commission (AEC), *Electoral Milestones for Women*; Buczynski-Lee, *When Mourning*, 2010 is Australia's foremost authority and filmmaker on Goldstein; also Bomford, *That Dangerous*, 1993; Goldstein, *Woman Suffrage*, 2008; Goldstein, *To America*, 2002; Henderson, *The Goldstein Story*, 1973; Women's Political Association, *The Life*, 1913.
17 AVAWA Secretariat, 'Trust the Women'.
18 Australian Government, National Archives, 'Australia's Prime Ministers'.
19 Bruley, *Women in Britain*, 1999, p. 24.
20 www.parliament.uk, *1913 Cat and Mouse Act*; Holt, *Magna Carta*, 2015, p. 94.
21 Smith, *Women's Suffrage Campaign*, 1998, 2007.
22 *Official Reports 5th Series: Commons*, 1912; following quotations this source.
23 Scutt, 'Police, Prosecution', 2011.
24 Manitoba – Digital Resources, 'Women Win'; A Country By Consent, *World War I*, 'Women'.
25 Stanton and Anthony Papers Project, 1997, vol. 1, chapter 23.
26 *Official Reports 5th Series: Commons*, 1912.
27 Jex-Blake, 'The medical education', 1987, p. 273.
28 Scutt, 'Wage rage', 2007.
29 National Library of Australia, *Trove*, 'Tailoresses Association'; Brooks, 'The Melbourne Tailoresses', 1983; Doolin, 'They will never crush!'
30 Bruley, *Women in Britain*, 1999, p. 22.
31 Defrancesco and Segal, 'Labour History', 2014.
32 Bruley, *Women in Britain*, 1999, p. 30.

DOI: 10.1057/9781137562357.0008

7
Bring Up the Bodies

Abstract: *Magna Carta proclaimed freemen could be imprisoned only by the law of the land. Husbands employed Blackstone's coverture rule to capture 'errant' wives. Yet as Scutt explains, Magna Carta worked for women: in 1891 habeas corpus freed Emily Jackson from her husband. Judges said she could leave him, and he could not imprison her. Yet Caroline Norton found habeas corpus could not release her children from a brutal husband's control. Nor, for centuries, did courts challenge Hale's infamous dictum that consent to marriage denies wives the right not to be raped. But 100 years after Jackson went free, over 750 years after Magna Carta, courts declared Hale wrong. Runnymede's barons and King John notwithstanding, Magna Carta's principle has made women's bodies (in this regard) at last their own.*

Keywords: Chief Justice Hale on rape; marital rape; rape in marriage; women's bodily integrity; women and child custody; women and children's rights; women and habeas corpus

Scutt, Jocelynne A. *Women and Magna Carta: A Treaty for Rights or Wrongs?* Basingstoke: Palgrave Macmillan, 2016. DOI: 10.1057/9781137562357.0009.

> No freemen shall be taken or imprisoned or disseised or exiled or
> in any way destroyed, nor will we go upon him nor send upon him,
> except by ... the law of the land.
>
> *Magna Carta, cap. 39*

Of the bodies of wives

On a Sunday afternoon in 1891, accompanied by one of her sisters, Emily
Emma Maude Jackson, nee Hall, worshipped at a church in Clitheroe,
Lancashire. Situated in Roger de Poitou country, Clitheroe has direct
links through Poitou to the Norman Conquest and the Angevin kings.
Poitou's landholdings extended through Salfordshire, Essex, Suffolk,
Nottinghamshire, Derbyshire, Lincolnshire, Hampshire and North
Yorkshire, parts of England fomenting much of the unrest fuelling the
13th-century barons' challenge to the king's power. Parts of the royal
forests featuring in Magna Carta and the negotiations leading to it lay in
Lancashire.

Dying in the middle of the 12th century around the time of Henry II's
accession to the throne, Poitou could not have anticipated the barons'
1214–1215 rebellion. Despite disgruntlement during Stephen's reign,
Magna Carta and its impact were for the future. Yet it was from Poitou
country that Emily Jackson was to test Magna Carta's declaration against
unlawful imprisonment. The calm of the Clitheroe church pew was not
to stay with her for long.

On 5 November 1887, Emily Jackson (at forty-two years a 'woman
of independent means') married Edmund Haughton Jackson. On 9
November 1887, Jackson executed a settlement of Emily's property,
including a benefit to himself of £5.0s.0d. weekly. The following day he
sailed for Aotearoa/New Zealand. Six months later, Emily was intended
to join him.[1]

Throughout 1888, Jackson enjoined Emily to sail for Port Wellington.
Now living with her sisters and brother-in-law, all implicated in the
unfolding drama, she implored him to return to England. Eventually,
he capitulated. Upon his arrival, Emily declined to live with him, even
refusing to see him. Jackson spent succeeding months importuning her
with letters. Emily remained incommunicado. He forced himself into
the family home, frightening Emily as she listened from the staircase to

DOI: 10.1057/9781137562357.0009

his tirade. Finally, asserting her siblings were denying his access, Jackson initiated action for restitution of conjugal rights. The decree issued. Emily disobeyed the order. Jackson chose direct action.

In *R. v. Jackson* (1891), Lord Esher, MR, graphically described events. The entire congregation witnessed Jackson, his friend Dixon Robinson, and a young lawyer's clerk seize Emily Jackson from the church:

> The wife is taken by the shoulders and dragged into a carriage, and falls on the floor of the carriage with her legs hanging out of the door. These have to be lifted in by ... the clerk. Her arm is bruised in the struggle. She is then driven off to the husband's house, the lawyer's clerk riding in the carriage with them. Could anything be more insulting?[2]

Even getting her into the carriage required 'separating her from her sister, to whom she was clinging ...'. At the house, she was 'placed ... in charge of [Jackson's] sister [having] instructions to give her every attention'. Despite her suffering no illness, a nurse and the lawyer's clerk remained 'obviously ... there to keep watch over her and control her ...'. Jackson ordered a doctor's visit, saying his wife's affections had been 'alienated from him' under her relations' influence.

Capturing Emily did not improve matters. Following the carriage, family members gathered outside Jackson's Blackburn house. Reporters arrived. Newspaper stories generated supporters and detractors. Police were called. A prosecution against Jackson for assaulting Emily's sister commenced. Jackson locked the house against all comers (bar the doctor), including police attending to execute the arrest warrant. Once, the blinds of a room Emily occupied were lowered sharply to prevent signals from family and supporters in the street. Later the blinds were raised, with 'no restraint ... upon her so seeing or communicating with her relations': communicating, presumably, by shouting (unlikely taking into account social constraints) or semaphore.

Jackson argued that having assisted him seize his wife, Dixon and the clerk remained to prevent 'a forcible rescue'. He claimed to have been kind:

> ... she had free run of the house, doing just as she pleased, save leaving [it]; ... he ... offered several times to take her for a drive, but she ... declined to go ...

The doctor said she complained only of a hurt arm and seizure of her bonnet which was thrown into the fire. (Emily Jackson later spoke of severe bruising and choking by the bonnet's ribbons as it was dragged from her head.)

DOI: 10.1057/9781137562357.0009

On appeal from Cave and Jeune, JJ., Lords Halsbury, LC, Esher, MR, and Fry, LJ heard argument on authorities, including jurists Blackstone, of the *Commentaries* (1765) endorsing coverture as advantaging women, Hale, of *Pleas of the Crown* (1736) endorsing the noose for witches, *Bacon's Abridgement* (c1760) distinguishing 'confinement' (a husband's entitlement) and 'imprisonment' (illegal), and cases, past and contemporary. Jackson's counsel placed considerable reliance on *In re Cochrane* (1840) where a husband legally defied his wife's request for release, with the judge saying a husband had, by law, 'power and dominion over his wife' to 'keep her by force within the bounds of duty'. This allowed beating, 'but not in a violent or cruel manner'.[3]

Declining to pursue that aspect, counsel said a husband's right to 'custody and control of his wife...to detain her by force if she refuses to live with him' remained. But, said Halsbury, if the past dictates that a husband who beats his wife is wrong, aren't propositions that he could imprison her equally wrong? Counsel cited Hale for the right to 'admonish and confine her to the house in case of the wife's extravagance'. Esher said that if a wife 'continues to refuse to live with the husband the confinement may be perpetual'. Counsel sidestepped, observing that a husband may not gain his wife's body by writ of habeas corpus, where she has voluntarily left him and, under no constraint, 'by her own desire' remains apart.

Though not explicitly posing it, Emily Jackson's counsel positioned wives as Magna Carta 'freemen':

> A husband has no power by the law of England to imprison his wife if she refuses to live with him. Every confinement is an imprisonment by law, whether it be to one room or one house. The [husband's] contention...would result in the reintroduction into society of private war.[4]

In reflecting Magna Carta, 'wholly untenable propositions' advanced for Jackson were contested:

> First,...that the husband may take possession of the wife's person by force, though no process of law could give him such possession of her. There never was any process of law for seizing and handing over the wife to the husband.

The judges agreed unanimously.

Fry addressed Jackson's proposition in two parts, 'the right to capture', and 'the right to confine'. Regarding the first, 'no rag of authority [favours] such a right'. *Cochrane's Case* was unfounded. Isolated in 1840

DOI: 10.1057/9781137562357.0009

and involving '[a husband's] right...to confine or imprison the wife until she rendered conjugal rights', no authority supported it before or since. *Bacon's Abridgement's* proposition that a husband 'has power and dominion over the wife, and may keep her by force within the bounds of duty' was 'so vague...it cannot be considered satisfactory authority'. It directly contradicted *R. v. Lister* (1721) where the court ordered a wife's release, saying he could restrain her only if she were 'spending his estate and consorting with lewd company'. As for imprisonment, no husband could, said Fry, 'enforce...restitution [of conjugal rights] by...imprisoning the wife'.[5] A husband would be 'at once a party, the judge, and the executioner', unacceptable and unlawful. (Though Fry didn't say it, this was Magna Carta barons' complaint against the king.)

For Esher: 'It is not and never was the law of England that the husband has...a right of seizing and imprisoning the wife'.[6] Halsbury agreed, saying if a distinction between 'imprisonment' and 'confinement' existed, here, 'there was imprisonment'. No husband could lawfully 'seize [his wife's] person...by force and detain her in his house until she be willing to restore to him his conjugal rights'. In 'refusing to go to and continue in her husband's house', Emily Jackson exercised free will, under no compulsion nor 'induced by anyone to refuse to continue' in Jackson's house, nor 'compelled to remain where she was before he removed her'. No court had ever had power to seize and despatch a wife to a husband, and the Matrimonial Causes Court no longer had power to imprison a wife refusing to obey a restitution of conjugal rights decree. Contentions that a husband had the right were wrong: none such exists nor ever did exist.

Suffering violent indignity from her husband, Emily Jackson had 'ample ground...to apprehend violence in the future'. Her liberty 'must be restored'. Magna Carta applied. Emily Jackson went free.

Of the bodies of children

With *R. v. Jackson*, a mooted House of Lords appeal came to nothing. For women like EC Wolstenholme Elmy, 'The Decision in the Clitheroe Case' (1891) spelled liberty. Others considered that it consolidated the law against women's interests, leaving women subjugated – though not entirely. Letters to the Editor generally supported Jackson. Dissatisfaction amongst 'husband right' supporters simmered. Returning home to her

DOI: 10.1057/9781137562357.0009

sister, Emily was shouted at and threatened. Meanwhile for women as mothers, habeas corpus had another side.[7]

Fifty years before, Caroline Sheridan Norton's husband George refused to let her see or communicate with their children. *Separation of Mother and Child* (1838) recounts her sudden realisation of erroneous assumptions that 'every mother has a *right* to the custody of her child till it attain the age of seven years.'[8] Father's legal rights were 'absolute and paramount', a mother non-existent. If she hid the children from their father (just as Norton hid them from her), he could by habeas corpus writ demand their return. Every court would support him. If she disobeyed, a court could imprison her. A mother's quality of care, nurture before birth and care for the children after birth were ignored. That a father was uncaring, incapable of parenting or providing proper nurture was irrelevant. He could commit adultery, live with a paramour, gamble, frequent houses of ill-frame, accost prostitutes on the street, or drink himself into a stupor whether in a common pub or an elite men's club. Mothers had no rights. This, said Norton, supported 'an individual right so entirely despotic', that the power can be – and has been – 'grossly and savagely abused... made the means of persecution, and the instrument of vengeance', with 'scarcely any degree of cruelty... not [having] been practised under colour of its protection'.

Norton died in 1877. Fourteen years later, judges and counsel in *R. v. Jackson* (1891) distinguished between wives and children, confirming father's right. Fry cited *R. v. Leggat* (1852) where Lord Campbell, CJ said a husband 'has no such custody of the wife as a parent has of a child'.[9] Emily Jackson's counsel confirmed this, saying a husband 'has no such right at common law to the custody of his wife' but a parent 'has a right to the custody of the child', so if a child 'be of tender years, the court will make an order for its restoration to him'. In using the gender specific 'him', her counsel struck at the heart of the problem confronting Norton and all married women when engulfed by child custody and access disputes.

A lengthy history of common law authority separated Norton from her children. In *De Manneville v. De Manneville* (1804) the Court of Chancery examined habeas corpus for Margaret De Manneville and her daughter Caroline Thomas De Manneville, a child of eleven months. A propertied woman, Margaret De Manneville had further expectations. Through their marriage settlement made in 1800, Leonard Thomas De Manneville's prospects were highly desirable, despite a clause that, being French, he:

DOI: 10.1057/9781137562357.0009

... should not at any time after the marriage by personal compulsion, or legal means, or by any other ways and means whatsoever compel or force his wife, contrary to her own free will and inclinations to reside in *France* or in any other country than *Great Britain*.[10]

Having left Manneville due to 'differences', from the nearby home of her mother's friend Margaret De Manneville advised him the child could be seen there. Unwell, she left Caroline with a nurse. Manneville seized the child. When Manneville was taken into custody as an alien, Margaret De Manneville recovered Caroline, moving to her mother's home. As Norton recounts, once released:

> ... wishing to compel a disposition of her property, [Manneville] entered by force the house where she had fled for refuge, dragged the child (which she was in the act of nursing) from the very breast; and took it away, almost naked, in an open carriage, in inclement weather ....[11]

Partially anticipating *R. v. Jackson* (1891) Lord Eldon, LC, observed that although Manneville had a right to possession of Margaret De Manneville and his child, the court had 'no authority' to 'deliver to [Manneville] the person of his wife'.[12] Manneville could institute a suit for restoration of conjugal rights, and if 'there [were] ill usage, that [would] justify her retiring from his residence', but Margaret De Manneville's remedy lay not in Chancery, but seeking separation through the Ecclesiastical Court. What about the child?

One account, *De Manneville v. De Manneville* (1806), had Margaret De Manneville 'obtain[ing] possession of the child by force and stratagem', while the father '... as far as was then shewn, had not abused his legal right, to the detriment of the infant ...'.[13] Possibly, 'force and stratagem' lay in Margaret De Manneville's leaving with the child. Still, the question remained: should the child be placed in her mother's custody, whose refusal to live with the father breached marriage contract obligations? The Ecclesiastical Court could, said Eldon, consider Manneville's religion and alien status, his 'coming here to propagate' 'despicable principles' contrary to the Alien Act. But none of that affected father's rights. In Chancery, the sole issue for custody was the child's possible removal from the country.

Affidavits describing the marital circumstances could not outweigh Margaret De Manneville's living in 'a state of actual, unauthorized, separation', seeking custody of the child whilst continuing in that separation, contrary to law. In past cases, Eldon said, he had removed a child from the father who was 'in constant habits of drunkenness and blasphemy,

DOI: 10.1057/9781137562357.0009

poisoning the mind of the infant'. But this gave the mother no rights.[14] Rather, 'due attention to parental authority, so abused, [was] to call in the authority of the King, as *Parens Patriae*' making the child a ward. As fathers alone had custodial rights, breach of parental duty meant a substitute father must be employed: king, not mother, replacing father. Hence, despite everything, Caroline was returned to Manneville, his only restraint an order 'not to remove the child from the kingdom'.

On 19 February 1805, Manneville returned to court. Called again on 10 March 1806, he had disappeared – presumably with the child, giving no security for the order he remain in the country. Margaret De Manneville and her (lack of) rights were not mentioned. Even had Manneville taken the child 'by fraud or violence', the court lacked power to 'take it away from him'.[15]

Ball v. Ball (1827) was equally firm. Mrs Ball and her daughter of fourteen, Emily Owen Ball, 'prayed that [she] might be placed under the mother's care', Mrs Ball bearing all expenses. Access 'at all convenient times' was put as an alternative. As with Caroline Norton, Mrs Ball's lawyers fought the matter of access and custody, recognising that realistically (and legally) father-right trumped all, at least with mothers and custody.

Emily Ball originally lived with her mother, visiting her father occasionally. On one visit, she was sent to boarding school without notice or advice to her mother of her whereabouts. The court compared both homes. At her father's house, company was a female servant. At her mother's, she had her mother's attention, 'who has always endeavoured to impress upon the child a proper regard towards [her father]'. In law, this meant nothing. Nor did Ball's adulterous relationship or Mrs Ball's divorce through the Ecclesiastical Court as the innocent party. Vice chancellor Sir Anthony Hart 'unless the father brings the child into contact with the woman', it was all irrelevant. 'Some conduct' on his part of 'management and education of the child' must be shown 'to warrant an interference with his legal right'. Despite 'in a moral point of view' knowing 'of no act more harsh or cruel than depriving the mother of proper intercourse with her child', Hart dismissed the petition.[16]

Separation of Mother and Child (1838) affirms this double standard of sex morality – not only tolerated but generated and supported by the law. 'Does *nature*,' Norton asked:

> ... say that the woman, enduring for nearly a year a tedious suffering, ending in an agony which perils her life, has no claim ... [T]hat the woman, who after that year of suffering is over, provides from her own bosom the nourishment

DOI: 10.1057/9781137562357.0009

[preserving] the very existence of her offspring, has no claim ... And that the whole and sole claim rests with him, who has slept while she watched ...? No![17]

Even where a man was bankrupt, his wife and mother 'forced to live separate from him [through] ill treatment', the child 'like to receive an improper education with her father, and ... not well used', for these mothers Magna Carta and habeas corpus provided no hope. In *Ex parte M'Clellan* (1831) Lord Mansfield did not dismiss a father's habeas corpus writ. He admonished the parties to agree saying, if they failed, he would decide what's best for the child, fixing upon a school. Mother-right had no place – again father-right bowed to *parens patraie* or court edict only. Even with wards of the court, as *In re Agar-Ellis* (1883) affirmed, excepting gross moral turpitude, abdication of paternal authority, or seeking to remove wards of court out of the jurisdiction without consent, a father's paternal authority was secure.[18]

Only where the mother was dead, with sizeable property threatened or de facto custody passing to relatives, was an errant father denied habeas corpus. In *Wellesley v. Wellesley* [1828] (1829), William Wellesley was, through marriage, in receipt of substantial property and income. His profligacy led to his flight, with wife and children, to the Continent where (unbeknownst to his wife) he commenced a long-term liaison with one Mrs Bligh. Whilst living in Italy, then Paris, subterfuge continued. Upon realising, Catherine Wellesley left, taking the children to England. Shortly after, she died, leaving the children with her family. Having returned surreptitiously with Mrs Bligh, Wellesley reappeared. Refused when demanding custody of the children, he sought habeas corpus.

Strong exception was taken to Wellesley's conduct in its entirety. Not only did he engage in 'immoral conduct' with Bligh and other women. 'One of the strongest reasons' going to 'custody and care of his children was:

> [H]e (as ... alleged) had deliberately accustomed them to profane swearing and the use of the lowest most vulgar slang; ... in his letters to the male infants he employed such expressions as ... : 'If the fellow be a sportsman who told you you could not hunt your harriers till next year, *d—n his internal soul to hell*', – and 'play hell and tommy; make as much row as your lungs will admit of; chase cats, dogs, women, young and old, etc. etc. ...[19]

Wellesley 'often expressed his intention to let the male infants associate with children of the lowest society and habits', told them 'swearing

DOI: 10.1057/9781137562357.0009

is a remedy against lying' and 'debauch all the ladies, young and old'.
He would ensure the children's presence 'at bull-baits, cock-fights and
all other sports of like nature,... [enabling] them to hear and learn oaths
and blasphemous language ...'. His 'particular wish' was that they 'should
adopt the manners and language of the lowest classes, [to] attain a knowledge of the world ...'. He 'boasted he had procured children of the lowest
description to come to the back of his [Paris] house' so they would 'teach
his children to repeat oaths and blasphemous language made use of by
such vagabonds, and... made his boys teach them to swear in English,
etc. etc'. Wellesley's application was lost.

Yet habeas corpus might advantage children – male children. Hence,
where a child of fourteen years lived with his aunt, the father seeking
habeas corpus to obtain possession of him, in *King v. Penelope Smith*
(1736) the judge refused to determine guardianship rights, setting the
child free to 'go where he thought fit'.[20] However, *In re Agar-Ellis* (1883)
the joint mother-daughter application for habeas corpus was refused.
Agar-Ellis restricted communication between his seventeen-year-old
daughter (a ward of the court) and her mother. His belief that contact
would alienate the daughter's affections from him prevailed.

Certainly unmarried mothers did succeed – whether claiming habeas
corpus to recover a child, or defending against habeas corpus and a
man asserting father right, or (in *The King v. Hopkins and Wife* (1806)) as
against an adopting couple, consent not being granted fully and freely.
Norton's *Separation of Mother and Child* expressed this keenly as an injustice, although at the time the right availed women little.[21] For unmarried
mothers, jobs were few, life on the street possibly the 'best' option, social
stigma labelling 'bastard children' and their mothers as shameful outsid-
ers. Kings were different. Before and after Magna Carta, a king's out-of-
wedlock children had status and his status suffered nothing. John's many
illegitimate children had advantages 'common bastards' lacked.

Of the bodies of wives and women

For women as mothers, legislative intervention was necessary. Norton
was influential. The Matrimonial Causes Act 1857 enabled women to
be freed legally from vicious husbands, at least in theory and under
limited circumstances. Divorce reform gave husbands more rights than
wives, and mothers' parental rights took longer to gain.[22] Legislation

DOI: 10.1057/9781137562357.0009

reversed absolute denial of mother's rights, yet not until the late 20th century did custody and residence, access and visitation laws make parents – male and female – equally responsible, at least formally, for children's care, wellbeing and financial upkeep.[23] Ironically, with reforms negating distinctions between legitimate and illegitimate children and social stigma for unwed mothers waning, the advantage Norton identified for unwed mothers was lost. Access to child and parent benefits and better-paid jobs meant women could bear children independently and support them. Paradoxically, unwed fathers gained rights akin to husbands – an equal 'say' in children's lives. Albeit possessing economic freedom, women could not escape masculine control by propagating out of wedlock.

Nor could women escape masculine control of their bodies. In enabling Emily Jackson to be free of a husband keeping her captive, Magna Carta should have enabled all married women to be free of husbands proclaiming possession of their bodies through coition. *Hale's Pleas of the Crown* (1736) was again a stumbling block, compounded by *East's Treatise* (1803) and *Archbold's Pleading* (1822). Hale's infamous contention, on his authority alone, averred that husbands could not be guilty of wife-rape, for:

> ... by their mutual matrimonial consent and contract the wife hath given up herself in this kind unto her husband which she cannot retract.[24]

In *R. v. R.* [1992] the House of Lords cited *Popkin v. Popkin* (1794) as supporting Hale: there, fifty-eight years after Hale's *Pleas* was published, in a 'separation from bed and board' case Lord Howell said a husband 'has a right to the person of his wife', adding 'but not if her health is endangered'.[25] This hardly confirms Hale, as it relies solely on Hale – making the argument circular. Alternatively, its ambiguity could refute Hale. Sexual intercourse without consent – in other words, rape – impacts physically and psychologically upon a woman's wellbeing, wife or not. Hence, *Popkin v. Popkin* might equally be read as supporting the proposition that rape in marriage is never lawful: always 'her health *will be* endangered'. Nonetheless, the Hale dictum implanted itself in the judicial wisdom of all common law countries: none was immune. This same judicial wisdom determining (apart from *Edwards v. Attorney General of Canada* [1929]) women were not persons, perhaps this was not surprising.[26]

Nevertheless, individual judges contested the 'not persons' ukase, and this followed for wife rape also. *R. v. Clarence* (1888), three years before

Emily Jackson was set free, was routinely but wrongly cited as supporting Hale. The case was not framed as rape, anyway. Two House of Lords
judges unequivocally rejected Hale (Wills and Field), one agreed with
Wills and Stephen (Coleridge), three said a married woman could resist
or were equivocal (Hawkins – with whom Day 'emphatically' agreed,
and Smith), Mathew, Manisty and Huddleston agreed with Stephen,
saying nothing on the point or being equivocal; Stephen said nothing on
it except that in his *Digest of the Criminal Law* (1877 edn) he rejected Hale,
in a later edition withdrawing that footnote. Alone, Pollock, B. supported
Hale without demur.[27]

Frances Power Cobbe's 'Wife Torture in England' (1878) generated
action against marital crimes. Harriet Taylor Mill, and Mill's parliamentary support did not help, although some decisions acknowledged
wives' rights not to be beaten, often honoured in the breach by husbands
and courts. In the 20th century, recognition of de facto relationships as
socially acceptable presaged an added danger: contentions that 'marital
rape immunity' (so called) should extend to them.

The principle of 'a woman's body is her own' was pursued into 20th-
century campaigns for abortion rights, pregnancy support and maternal
health – never issues for Magna Carta, but through the proposition
consistent with Holt's 'adaptability' principle and Beloff's 'living law',
'rights' should mean 'for women, too'.[28] Underpinning these claims was
a philosophy of women's equality and personhood, although women's
organisations were not always or indeed ever ad idem. As with the struggle for the vote, entry to public office, legislatures and courts, equal pay,
cooperation and sisterhood, matters of the body generated splits and
division. Whether Canada's 'Famous Five', the five women recognised as
persons through *Edwards v. A-G of Canada* [1929], would see their Privy
Council win as affirming women's bodily integrity is unclear. History
affirms their limitations in not favouring minority background or Native
American women's rights, and elsewhere, whilst parts of the Women's
Movement endorsed *all* women's rights, freedom from slavery and servi-
tude others vocally disagreed.[29]

Marital rape and all women's freedom from sexual imposition were
pronounced sites of the struggles in the 1970s and 1980s. Laws changed in
Australia, North America and Aotearoa/New Zealand. Virginia Blomer
Nordby led the 1974 Michigan campaign, propelling major legislative
overhaul, yet rape in marriage initially covered separated couples only.
By 1990 all fifty states had legislated against marital rape, though not

DOI: 10.1057/9781137562357.0009

necessarily recognising wives' rights as equal to unmarried rape victims/ survivors, some requiring threat or force, not simply lack of consent. South Australian law changed in 1976, though politics watered down the marital rape clause. In 1981 New South Wales was first to make marriage irrelevant to rape prosecutions. Canada's reforms came in 1983, whilst Aotearoa/New Zealand passed major reforms in 1987.[30]

The UK effected some change,[30] yet 'rape in marriage' remained frozen in 1636. Whilst clinging to Hale, courts eventually acknowledged that a divorced or separated husband raping his wife could be prosecuted. Yet not until *R. v. R.* (1991) did the House of Lords concede Hale no longer controlled women's lives – at least for marital rape. The Australian High Court concluded likewise in *R. v. L.* (1991) then in *PGA v. The Queen* (2012) trounced Hale when PGA, prosecuted for raping his wife in 1963 – prior to 1970s reforms, challenged his conviction unsuccessfully.

Ironic that precisely 100 years lay between *R. v. Jackson* and *R. v. R.* If, as *R. v. Jackson* (1891) held, a woman could not be caught, trapped, confined, imprisoned by her husband despite the law's provision that marriage carries with it cohabitation – meaning, the wife to cohabit with the husband, following him wherever he might go – wouldn't it logically ensue that if marriage carries with it conjugal rights, a husband is disentitled from enforcing them should his wife not agree? The courts and counsel did not develop this import of *R. v. Jackson*. Yet as an adaptable and 'living law', Magna Carta affirms: No freewoman shall be taken ... except by the law of the land.

Nor shall any man have a right to his wife's person. Her person, herself, belongs to her. Though they did not say so, echoing *Edwards v. A-G of Canada* [1929], the House of Lords, like the Australian High Court, at last made married women persons.

Notes

1   Newspapers ran extensive stories, Jackson published *The True Story*, 1891; Emily Jackson's five-part 'Vindication' appeared in *Lancashire Evening Post* and *Times*. Bibbings, *Binding Men*, 2014, includes newspaper and journal coverage; also Kasem, 'Looking for Law', 2003–2004. .
2   *R. v. Jackson* (1891), at 683; following quotations this source, at 672, 674, 675–676. 677; Emily Jackson's recitation: Bibbings, *Binding Men*, 2014.
3   *Re Cochrane* (1840), at 631.

DOI: 10.1057/9781137562357.0009

4   *R. v. Jackson* (1991), at 677; following quotation this source, 677.

5   *R. v. Jackson* (1991), at 686 (Fry); following quotation this source, at 686 (Fry); 684 (Esher), 680 (Halsbury), 678 Halsbury). Fry (685) acknowledged resort to Ecclesiastical Courts for restitution of conjugal rights, not capture and confinement.

6   Bibbings, *Binding Men*, 2014.

7   Norton, *Separation*, 1838; reprinted nd, pp. 2, 3.

8   *R. v. Jackson* (1891), at 685 per Fry, LJ; at 678 (Emily Jackson's counsel); following quotation at 678 (Emily Jackson's counsel).

9   *De Manneville v. De Manneville* (1804), at 763.

10   Norton, *Separation*, 1838, p. 4.

11   *De Manneville v. De Manneville* (1804), at 765; following quotations this source, at 766, 768.

12   *De Manneville v. De Manneville* (1804), at 766, 768; *De Manneville* (1806), at 80.

13   *De Manneville v. De Manneville* (1804), at 766.

14   *De Manneville v. De Manneville* (1804), at 766, 768.

15   *Ball v. Ball (1)* (1827), at 485–486.

16   Norton, *Separation*, 1838, pp. 9–10.

17   See also *Blissets Case* (1774).

18   *Wellesley v. Wellesley* [1828], at 484; following quotations *Wellesley v. Wellesley* (1829), at 236, 249.

19   Norton, *Separation*, 1838, p. 72.

20   Norton, *Separation*, 1838, p. 1.

21   Radi, 'Whose Child', 1979; Elmy, *A Collection of Pamphlets*, 1883.

22   *Family Law Act* 1975 (Cth) equalises financial responsibilities, too; for UK see Welstead and Edwards, *Family Law*, 2013.

23   Hale, *Pleas of the Crown*, 1736, p. 629. Like others, *Archbold's Pleading*, 1822, p. 259 reiterates Hale, *Stephen's Digest of the Criminal Law* doubted Hale: 1877 edn, p. 172, subsequently withdrawn: *R. v. Clarence* (1888).

24   *Popkin v. Popkin* (1794), 765n.

25   Marital rape as 'no crime', Canada: Koshan, *The Legal Treatment*, nd; North America: Hodgson and Kelley, *Sexual Violence*, 2002; UK: Edwards, *Sex and Gender*, 1996, 2013; Australia: Scutt, *The Incredible Woman*, 1996; Scutt, *Women and the Law*, 1990; Aotearoa/New Zealand: Simpkin, 'Rape Law Reform, 1987; common law countries: Adamo, 'The Injustice', 1989.

26   See Scutt, 'Consent in Rape', 1977.

27   Holt, *Magna Carta*, 2015, p. 34; Beloff, 'Magna Carta', 2015, p. 6.

28   See Sharpe and McMahon, *The Persons Case*, 2007.

29   Nordby, 'Rape Law Reform', 1980; Gender Bias and the Law Project, *Heroines of Fortitude*, 1996; Roberts and Gebotys, 'Reporting Rape Laws', 1995; McDonald and Tinsley (eds), *From 'Real Rape' to Real Justice*, 2011.

30   Edwards, *Sex and Gender*, 1996, 2013.

DOI: 10.1057/9781137562357.0009

8
Conclusion – Claiming Magna Carta Rights

Abstract: *Scutt celebrates women's strength and will in renouncing subservience as their lot, just as the 1215 barons refused to accept tyranny. Ironically, she notes, although the US Constitution took Magna Carta as its foundation, US women effectively referencing it in their 1848 Seneca Fall claims and subsequently, Canada, Aotearoa/New Zealand, the UK and Australia beat the US to a woman as national leader. Scutt notes, too, the impact of women from smaller, less populous west coast states or provinces, their abilities and capabilities better recognised, men's power less entrenched. Today, US women reassert a right to an Equal Rights Amendment (ERA) affirming women's right to equality. Scutt confirms women's continuing demand for women as persons entitled to rights Magna Carta should and now may advance.*

Keywords: Equal Rights Amendment (ERA); Seneca Falls Convention 1848; women and freedom; women as president; women as prime minister; women's Magna Carta rights; women's rights campaigns

Scutt, Jocelynne A. *Women and Magna Carta: A Treaty for Rights or Wrongs?* Basingstoke: Palgrave Macmillan, 2016.
DOI: 10.1057/9781137562357.0010.

> We have … granted to all the freemen of our kingdom, for us and
> our heirs in perpetuity, all the below written liberties, to be had and
> held by them and their heirs from us and our heirs.
>
> *Magna Carta 1215*

Magna Carta – dead, alive, indifferent?

Despite protestations of perpetuity, Magna Carta 1215 had an initially
short life. Almost immediately, fearing he had conceded too much too
readily and sensing a continuing baronial dissatisfaction, disloyalty and
lust for power, John repudiated it. Secretly, he contacted the Pope who
by bull of 24 August (arriving in England in October) asserted the agreement was 'shameful, demeaning, illegal, unjust and harmful to royal
rights and the English people'. It was 'null and void of all validity for
ever'. Civil war began. Shortly after, John died of dysentery. Nine-year-
old Henry III came to the throne. As regent, through swift manoeuvring
and prowess in battle, albeit in his seventies, William Marshall recovered
London, lost by John to French Louis and rebel barons. Defeated, Louis
returned to France.[1]

With Henry III's accession, Magna Carta 1216 and 1217 were sealed,
then Magna Carta 1225, each fashioned on its predecessor. Again, no
women participated. Although not without stamina and the trappings of
power their status might bring, noble women were nonetheless absent by
name, their place wholly relational to men – as sisters, daughters, wives.
That secondary status, the absence of women as identities, much less as
signatories, affirms personhood was denied to them.

So, does it matter? If women weren't there, played no part, had little
or no acknowledged stake, do masculine posturing and Machiavellian
contrivance, or assertions of long-lived rights matter? Have such time-
honoured principles counted even for men?

Rebellion, colonialism and women of the west

Some scholars say Magna Carta didn't signify for anyone, never mind
women. Overrated, its influence is exaggerated. Holt's authoritative
Magna Carta takes this view. So, in her chatty contribution to the *New*

DOI: 10.1057/9781137562357.0010

Yorker, 'The Rule of History', does history professor Jill Lepore – observing, as others, that Magna Carta was not 'new'. Preceded by the regular swearing of coronation oaths by kings, 'binding themselves to the administration of justice', the practice commenced in France in 877 with Louis II.[2]

Yet at Runnymede, the barons believed it 'meant something' as, clearly, did John. Otherwise why seek the Pope's imprimatur in its renunciation, or indeed renounce it at all? Perhaps its political impact is what has, ultimately, counted most. This is evident in the reverential stance taken in the US, where for an 800-year anniversary the American Bar Association extolled it as the 'icon of liberty under law'. In celebration, American lawyers converged on Runnymede to reflect and refurbish the ABA Memorial, erected in 1957.[3]

In 1776, when declaring independence from the British Empire and George III, the US saw Magna Carta as its foundation. When women met at Seneca Falls in 1848, taking their lead from the Declaration of Independence, they too affirmed a belief in Magna Carta's power. Women's sense of justice, arising from a recognition of the rights and wrongs of women more than the barons' concerns, led to women being written into 'official' US history, just as it has generated women's claims around the world. After all, omission from Magna Carta will have meant something to the women of the time: hardly to be expected that they sat wreathed in roses, smelling the lavender whilst the action was chanced at Runnymede. History tells us some women at least would have been incensed at their sole reference through patriarchal relations and relationships.

Certainly women have far more on which to build. Kempe (c. 1373–c. 1438), Pizan (1364–c. 1430), Wollstonecraft (1759–1797) had their precursors – 13th-century novelist Heldris of Cornwall, 16th-century's playwright Aphra Bhen and writer Katherine (Kateryn) Parr, 18th-century's poet Anne Finch and philosopher Mary Astell, and more not yet unearthed.[4] As Ruth Bader Ginsberg said on 10 August 1993, upon her inauguration as Supreme Court justice, women build on foremothers' energies and intellect:

> I would not be in this room today if it were not for the dreams of women and men, dreams they kept alive when no one else would listen. Susan B. Anthony, Elizabeth Cady Stanton and Harriet Tubman come to mind. I stand on the shoulders of those brave people ...[5]

DOI: 10.1057/9781137562357.0010

Anthony (1820–1906), Stanton (1815–1902) and Tubman (c.1822–1913) were born on the US east coast. Yet women's activism so often developed and grew from the west. Western states, first Wyoming in 1869, gained the women's vote long before states in the east acceded. In Canada similarly: Manitoba women won the vote first, on 28 January 1916, with Saskatchewan and Alberta following on 14 March and 19 April respectively, then British Columbia on 5 April 1917, beating Ontario to voting rights by seven days. In Australia, South Australia (1894) preceded Western Australia (1899), and the late 19th century saw Western Australia constituting all-women Australian Labor Party (ALP) branches, Labor stalwart Jean Beadle (1868–1942) travelling around the south-west recruiting women members. Western Australia produced the first Australian women parliamentarian: Edith Cowan, in 1921 displacing a sitting attorney-general; first female Labour parliamentarian in the world, May Holman, elected in 1925; Florence Cardell-Oliver, appointed minister for health in October 1949, first Australian woman attaining full cabinet rank; first woman in the Senate, Labor's Dorothy Tangney (1911–1985); and in 1990 first female premier, Labor's Carmen Lawrence. Perhaps the smaller population in the west and a consequent lesser stranglehold by men over positions of authority and power propelled women into asserting their authority with a correspondingly better outcome.[6]

Although the first woman elected to the Australian lower house, Enid Lyons (1943, the same year as Tangney), was from Tasmania, an eastern state, low population numbers possibly generated the same women's assertiveness, less entrenched male power, and possibly greater readiness, through sheer necessity, to accept women (although not without struggle) as more equal, at least for a time.[7]

It was women of the west, too – dubbed Canada's 'Famous Five' – who finally persuaded judges that women are persons. Paradoxically, *Edwards v. A-G of Canada* [1929] was decided by the Privy Council – for Canada a bastion of conservatism. Earlier, in the 1890s, in vying for nationhood, Australia too sought escape from the Privy Council's hold. However, writing it out of the proposed Constitution and writing in Australia's High Court for final appeals was rejected. By the Commonwealth of Australia Constitution Act 1900, Westminster put it back.

Whatever their original roots, the Privy Council's first 'persons' were of the west in outlook and connections. Born in England, the daughter of an English colonial officer, Irene Marryat Parlby (1868–1965) was no

DOI: 10.1057/9781137562357.0010

less 'west' than her *Edwards'* co-litigants. Marriage took her to Alberta
and United Farm Women's Association (UFWA) activism, with a seat
in Alberta's legislative assembly, the second woman in Canada and
the Empire elevated to cabinet. Emily Murphy (1868–1933), principal
persons' case protagonist, was the first woman appointed as magistrate in
the British Empire – the post in Alberta. Henrietta Edwards (1849–1931),
born in Montreal, went west with her husband, later moving with him to
the North West Territories: active in the Women's Christian Temperance
League (WCTU) and National Council of Women (NCW), she pressed
women's causes from this remoteness, lending her name and energies
to the 'women's personhood' demand. Playing premier in a Women's
Parliament run by the Political Equality League immediately before
Manitoba women won the vote, Nellie Mooney McClung (1873–1951)
joined the 'persons' fight with alacrity, as did Louise Crummy McKinney
(1868–1931): born in Ontario, she taught in North Dakota then moved to
a small town west of Calgary. She, too, went with her husband; she, too,
advanced women's activism through the WCTU.[8]

That the Privy Council took the stand it did has been attributed to
newly appointed lord chancellor, Lord Sankey's wish to make his mark.
Yet why this case, this way? The matter is more complex. Beginning life
as a Conservative, elected to London County Council in 1910, Sankey's
first judicial appointment came in 1914 through HH Asquith's Liberal
government. When David Lloyd George appointed him head of the
1919 coal mining industry inquiry, Sankey became alert to the ravages
wrought on miners, their tough industrial conditions and mine owners'
greed: he recommended nationalisation. This radically changing political perspective generated friendships with Fabians Sydney and Beatrice
Webb and George Bernard Shaw. A strong women's rights supporter,
Shaw treasured Australian activist Vida Goldstein (1869–1949) as friend
and colleague. Her impact on Shaw – perhaps his model for St Joan
and influential in *Pygmalion* – cannot be underestimated. By the time
Sankey heard 'the persons' case' in 1929, opportunities for an expanding
consciousness of women's rights and wrongs were manifest.[9]

Sankey was one of five *Edwards* judges. Two judges, Lord Tomlin
and Sir Lancelot Sanderson, held no obviously indicative views. The
remaining two declared themselves in the rumbling dispute following
Viscountess Rhondda's claim [1922] for a seat in the Lords. During a 1924
debate one (Lord Darling) asked what 'grounds of logic or convenience'
admitted women to one house whilst barring them from the other?

DOI: 10.1057/9781137562357.0010

Surely if a woman might 'sit on the Throne', why not 'on these benches?'. In 1925, the second (Lord Merrivale) contributed by stressing 'feminist involvement', his shorthand for 'debate roundly scuppered'. Perhaps thoughts of Viscountess Rhonnda (1883–1958) were too raw, she having served time in the suffragette struggle, jumping on the running board of Asquith's car and posting a chemical bomb to destroy letters or demolish the box. Like Susan B. Anthony (1820–1906), Rhondda refused to pay a fine (£10) and was released only after her hunger strike lasted five days.[10]

Magna Carta flawed

Autonomous women's absence from Magna Carta is not its only failing. Sojourner Truth (c.1797–1883) recognised this implicitly when, at the 1851 Ohio Women's Rights Convention, she rebutted a man's lecturing against women's rights, declaring:

> That man ober there say that woman needs to be helped into carriages, and lifted ober ditches, and to have the best place everywhar. Nobody ever helps me into carriages or ober mud puddles, or gives me any best place! And ar'n't I a woman?[11]

Frances Dana Gage (1808–1884), chairing the convention, reported Truth's next words:

> Ar'n't I a woman? Look at me! Look at my arm! [Here she bared her right arm to the shoulder, showing her tremendous muscular power] I have ploughed, and planted, and gathered into barns, and no man could head me? And ar'n't I a woman? ...

Little wonder US independence did not acknowledge women's personhood, for in relying on Magna Carta, how could it? How, too, could it acknowledge the blot of slavery? Magna Carta was drawn by a civilisation approving it. As Lord Mansfield said in *Somerset v. Stewart* [1772], this was a practice and policy 'incompatible with the natural rights of mankind, and the principles of good government.' In 1215, villeins were Britain's slaves, owned by Magna Carta's barons.

Mansfield's decision that the slave James Somerset (no given name for him in the case report, nor salutation) should, when brought into Britain by his owner, Charles Stewart ('Mr Stewart' throughout), go free profoundly impacted in America's south. In *Rough Crossings*, Simon Schama argues Mansfield effectively drew southern and northern colonies together, joined in rebellion against George III. Southerners feared the freedom granted to Somerset might cross the Atlantic, despite Mansfield's explicit limitation of his finding to England. Had *Somerset v. Stewart* not been decided as it was, when it was, the American Revolution might never have happened.[12]

Despite the grand statement 'all men are born free and equal', many of those leading the American independence movement not only had wives, but owned slaves. George Washington and Thomas Jefferson, most often cited, were not alone. When news of Somerset's win in England reached the colonies, Jefferson had thirty slaves disappear, James Madison and Benjamin Harrison lost twenty apiece, Arthur Middleton 'mislaid' fifty, at least one of Washington's 'deserted' to loyalist lines, and Edward Rutledge, most junior of the Declaration's signatories, also lost slaves. These losses infected the claim for US sovereignty and a court system where *Somerset v. Stewart* had no sway. Not only, despite Abigail Adams' 1776 plea, did these fathers of freedom forget 'the ladies' but they also overlooked their inhumanity to man in ownership of women and men to whom they not only denied freedom, but bought and sold like cattle – just as husbands had bought and sold wives, denounced by spinsters as inhumanity to women.[13]

Still, there was more. With the decision that a state's population tally should determine how to calculate the number of representatives each state could return to the lower house of Congress, southern delegates wanted slaves counted. Northern delegates argued slaves were property, hence should not be considered. The compromise was for each slave to count as 3/5ths of a person.[14]

This disregard for humanity extended to Native Americans, ignored altogether, as it did to Indigenous Australians and Maori of Aotearoa/New Zealand.[15] Whether it is better to be counted as 3/5ths of a human being in North America or not counted at all as in the antipodes is a question that ought not exist. Ethnicity or race does not define a person's humanity, just as sex or gender does not define whether a human being is a person. Yet this ignorance occurred in countries asserting Magna Carta as a human rights foundation, albeit few of those to whom, today, it is presumed to extend were ever included or contemplated within its provisions.

DOI: 10.1057/9781137562357.0010

So where are the women?

When on 31 March 1776 Abigail Adams wrote to husband John, later US president, she observed that in making a 'new code of laws' he should 'remember the ladies and be more generous and favourable to them than [his] ancestors'. Acutely aware of history's limitations, she would have demanded Magna Carta be a living, not a static, rights charter. 'Do not put such unlimited power into the hands of the husbands', she pleaded. Her husband should 'remember, all men would be tyrants if they could'.

She then wrote the words manifest in future struggles of women for the rights – articulated by women at 1848 Seneca Falls, then 1851 Ohio, and down the decades and the centuries, across oceans and continents, mirroring the demands of women of the decades and the centuries before:

> If particular care and attention is not paid to the ladies, we are determined to foment a rebellion, and will not hold ourselves bound by any laws in which we have no voice or representation.[16]

Two centuries on, US women lobbied hard for an Equal Rights Amendment (ERA). The 19th Amendment for women's right to vote was not enough. Anthony's discovery in 1873 that the 1860s Civil War provisions applied to men only – including those once slaves – not to women, whether wives, former slaves or 'free', did not end with the vote. The ERA, proposed by Alice Paul (1885–1977), entered Congress in 1923, finally passed in 1972 for ratification, faltered after reaching thirty-five of the required thirty-eight states, and failed by the final 30 June 1982 deadline.

Recognising the common law continued to deny women real equality, the National Organisation of Women (NOW), other women's organisations and individual women promoted the ERA against conservative scaremongering based in assertions attributable to *Blackstone's Commentaries* (1765). Women backing it held the ERA essential to removing husbands' preferential treatment over wives, 'obsolete and irrational notions of chivalry' viewing women 'in a patronizing or condescending light' and fostering double standards extending greater sexual freedom to men than women. Magna Carta's flaws required a new constitutional safeguard, explicitly providing:

> Equality of rights under the law shall not be denied or abridged by the United States or by any State on account of sex.

DOI: 10.1057/9781137562357.0010

Reintroduced into Congress on 14 July 1982 and voted down a year later, this left women invidiously lacking equality and being denied unequivocal Bill of Rights protection, knowing Congress had reneged on its earlier acknowledgement of women as persons.[17]

Then, 800 years after Magna Carta, on 23 June 2015, Oscar-winning actor Meryl Streep wrote to all 535 members of Congress insisting they 'stand up for equality':

> ...for your mother, your daughter, your sister, your wife or yourself – by actively supporting the Equal Rights Amendment [for] equal pay, equal protection from sexual assault, equal rights.[18]

Although equality cannot be measured in women in high places and positions of power alone, 800 years on, the country trumpeting so roundly its Magna Carta allegiance awaited a woman leader. The UK, Aotearoa/New Zealand, Canada and Australia had elected women prime ministers – Margaret Thatcher (1979, 1983, 1987), Helen Clark (1999, 2002, 2005), Kim Campbell (1993), Julia Gillard (2010). Yet no country with Magna Carta in its history can stand sanguine. The slave James Somerset was set free 100 years before; in *R. v. Jackson* (1891), the wife Emily Jackson walked free from that Blackburn house where her husband held her. All Indigenous Australian women gained national voting rights some fifty years after their 'white' sisters. All Inuit, Asian and Aboriginal women finally gained the vote in 1960s Canada, forty years after all 'white' Canadian women.[19]

Is there, then, a future for women in Magna Carta? Do Magna Carta principles hold any further hope for women's assertions of equal status, equal rights and equal entitlements to law, justice, employment and equal pay, public office and bodily and psychic integrity?

Surely so long as women draw breath, whilst women demand meaningful lives, while women acknowledge the historical roots of women's struggle and make claims for the future for themselves, their daughters and granddaughters...so long as women stand defiant as persons, free women or freewomen will make Magna Carta speak for us all.

Notes

1   Carpenter, *Magna Carta*, 2015, pp. 401–402, ch. 12 'Enforcement', pp. 374–403, ch. 13 'Revival', pp. 404–429.

DOI: 10.1057/9781137562357.0010

2 Holt, *Magna Carta*, 2015; Holt, *Northerners*, 1992; Lepore, 'Rule of History', 2015.

3 American Bar Association, *Magna Carta 800*, 2015.

4 *The Aphra Behn Page*, 2011; Mueller, *Early Modern Englishwoman*, 1997; Heldris, *Silence*, 1992; Stanford Encyclopaedia, *Mary Astell*, 2005; Spender, *Women of Ideas*, revised edn, 1990.

5 Quoted Scutt (ed), *Living Generously*, 1996.

6 Joyce, 'Feminism', 1984; Joyce, 'Labor Women', 1986; Brown, 'Cowan, Edith Dircksey', 1981; Australian Government, 'Australian women', 2011.

7 Lyons, *Among the Carrion*, 1997.

8 Sharpe and McMahon, *Persons Case*, 2007; Susan Jackel, *Women's Suffrage*, 2013.

9 On Shaw and Goldstein, see Karen Buczynski-Lee, *When Mourning Becomes Electric*, research for MA (Film), 2011.

10 BBC News, 'Suffragette Viscountess Rhondda', 2013; Sharpe and McMahon, *Persons Case*, 2007, p. 172; House of Lords, *Hansard*, vol. 58, 1924, p. 711; House of Lords, *Hansard*, vol. 61, 1925, p. 45.

11 Gage, 'Ain't I a Woman'; following quotation that source.

12 Schama, *Rough Crossings*, 2006.

13 *This Day in History*, Abigail Adams urges husband.

14 United States House of Representatives, *House of Representatives, Origins & Development*.

15 Although all Maori men had voting rights in Aotearo/New Zealand (1867) before all European men (1879): Teara/Encyclopedia of New Zealand, *Story – Voting Rights*, http://www.teara.govt.nz/en/voting-rights (accessed 20 November 2015).

16 *This Day in History*, Abigail Adams urges husband.

17 House of Representatives, [1971]; Daughtrey, 'Women and the Constitution', 2000.

18 Oh, 'Meryl Streep Is Pushing Congress', 2015.

19 Susan Jackal, *Women's Suffrage*, 2013.

DOI: 10.1057/9781137562357.0010

List of Cases

In re Agar-Ellis (1883) Ch. 317, 109–10

In re Baby M, 537 A.2d 1227, 109 N.J. 396 (N.J. 02/03/1988)., 34

R. v. Bain [1992] 1 SCR 91, [1992] CanLII 111 (SCC), 52

Ball v. Ball (1) (1827) 2 Sim 33; ER 485, 108

Ballard v. United States 329 US 187 (1946), 51

Bank of Victoria Ltd v. Mueller (1925) VicLawRp 74; (1925) VLR 642, 85n7

Barclays Bank Plc v. O'Brien & Anor [1993] UKHL 6; [1994] 1 AC 180, 78, 80, 85n14, 85n16–17

Bebb v. Law Society (1913) B. 305; [1914] 1 Ch. 286, 49

Beresford-Hope v. Lady Sandhurst (1889) 23 QBD 79, 22

Bertha Cave's Case, The Times, 3 December 1903, 28

R. v. Biddle (1995) 96 CCC (3d) 323; [1995] CanLII 134 (SCC), 52, 53

Blissets Case (1774) Loft 748, 114n14

Bradwell v. The State of Illinois 83 US 130 (1872), 26, 27, 29

Brown v. Brown (1976) 9 ALR 368, 66

Brown v. Ingram (1868) 7 M. 281, 22, 27

Catharine v. Surry 7 Mod. 263

CES and Another v. Superclinics (Australia) Pty Ltd and Others (1995) 38 NSWLR 47, 37

Charman v. Charman [2007] EWCA Sev 503, 70n29

Chorlton v. Lings (1868–1869) LR 4 CP 374, 20, 38n14, 49, 54n19, 92

Re Cochrane (1840) 8 Dowl. 630, 104

Cole v. Van Riper (1861) 479 https://archive.org/stream/jstor-3303222/3303222_djvu.txt (accessed 19 May 2015), 61, 69n13

Craig v. Jex-Blake (1871) 9 M. 973, 23

Day v. Shaw and Shaw [2014] EWHC 36 (Ch), 85n16

Edwards v. AG of Canada (Reference re the Meaning of the Word 'Persons' in Section 24 of the British North America Act) [1928] SCR 276, 31

Edwards v. AG of Canada [1929] UKPC 86; [1930] AC 143, *Edwards
v. AG of Canada* [1930] AC 128 http://www.bailii.org/uk/cases/
UKPC/1929/1929_86.html (accessed 12 May 2015), 38, 50, 54n23

Fares v. Box Hill College of TAFE and Anor (1992) EOC ¶92–391, 72, 84n1

Flores v. Flores, 847 S.W. 2d 648 (Tex. App. Waco) (1993), 65

Garcia v. National Australia Bank Ltd [1998] HCA 48; 6 CCL 81; 194 CLR
395; 72 ALJR 1243 (6 August 1998), 80–81, 85n16, 85n19

Grigby v. Cox (1750) 27 ER 1178, 85n7

Margaret HS Hall (for admission to Law Agent's Examination) (1901) 9 SLT
150, 27; *Hall v. Incorporated Society of Law Agents (Miss Margaret HS
Hall)* (1901) No 171 Court of Sessions vol. 111 1059

Application of Kathleen May Harrigan (HCA, 10 June 1982, No S 34 of 1982,
unreported), 37

Hawke v. Smith No 1, 253 US 221 (1920), 96

Hawke v. Smith No 2, 253 US 231 (1920), 96

In re Edith Haynes (1904) 6 WALR 209, 28

Holt v. Lyle 1607, 19

Hoyt v. Florida 386 US 57 (1961), 51

JEB v. Alabama ex rel. TB 511 US 127 (1994), 51

Jex-Blake v. Senatus of University of Edinburgh (1873) 11 M. 784, 24, 54n17

Kane and Kane [2013] FamCAFC 205 (18 December 2013), 70n29

King v. Penelope Smith (1736) 2 Str. 982; (1736) Ridgeway Temp. Hardwicke
147; 27 ER 787, 110

The King v. Hopkins and Wife (1806) 7 East 577, 110

Re Kitson [1920] SASR 230, at 231, 33

Leves v. Haines (1986) EOC ¶92–167, 72, 84n2

Louth v. Diprose [1992] HCA 61; (1992) 175 CLR 621 (2 December 1992),
79–80

Ex parte M'Clellan (1831) 1 Dowl. 84, 109

De Manneville v. De Manneville (1804) 10 Ves. 762, 106, 114n8, 114n10–11

De Manneville v. De Manneville (1806) 12 Ves. 78, 107

Mason & Mason and Anor [2013] FamCA 424 (7 June 2013), 35

Nairn v. University of St Andrews and Edinburgh (1908) SC 113. 30

*Nairn & Ors v. University Courts of the Universities of St Andrews and
Edinburgh & Ors* (1906) 14 SLT 176, 30

Naylor v. Field, 5 Dutch 287, 69n13

Ex parte Ogden (1893) 16 NSWLR 86, 22

Olive v. Ingram (1738) 7 Mod. 263; 87 ER 1230; 2 Stra. 114; 93 ER 1067, 19, 21,
49, 93

PGA v. The Queen [2012] HCA 21, 113

Page v. Horne (1848) 11 Beav 227, at 235; 50 ER 804, at 807, 79–80

Palmer v. State of Indiana 197 Ind. 625, 150 NE 917 (1926), 50

Popkin v. Popkin (1794) 1 Hag. Ecc. 765n, 111

DOI: 10.1057/9781137562357.0011

Pybus v. Smith (1790) 30 ER 294, 85*n*7

R. v. Bayliss (1986) 9 Qld Lawyer Rep. 8, 37

R. v. Bain [1992] 1 SCR 91, 52

R. v. Biddle [1995] 1 SCR 761, 52–3

R. v. Catizone (1972) 23 CRNS 44 (Ont. Co.Ct), 51

R. (On the Application of the Fawcett Society) v. Chancellor of the Exchequer [2010] EWJC 3522 (Admin), 72, 82

R. v. Clarence (1888) 122 QBD 23, 111, 114*n*20

R. v. Davidson [1969] VR 667, 37

R. v. Jackson (1891) 1 QB 671, 103, 105–7, 113, 114*n*4, 123

R. v. Kokopenace (2015) SCC 28 (CanLII), 55*n*28

R. v. L. [1991] HCA 48; (1991) 174 CLR 379. 113

R. v. Leach and Brennan (2010) QDC (unreported), 37

R. v. Leggat (1852) 18 QB 781; 118 Eng.Rep. 295, 106

R. v. Lister (1721) 1 Stra. 477; 93 Eng.Rep. 645, 105

R. v. Morgantaler [1988] 1 SCR 30, 39*n*39

R. v. Napoose (No. 1) (1991) 85 AtlaLR (2d) 8 (Alta.QB), 51

R. v. R. [1992] 1 A.C. 599 (HL), 111, 113

Roe v. Wade, 410 US 113 (1973), 36

R. v. Wald (1971) 3 DCR (NSW) 25, 37

Semayne v. Berisford (Seymane's Case) (1604) 5 co Rep 91A; [1558–1774] All ER 62; 15 Digest (Rep) 978, 58

Slaughter House Cases 83 US 36 (1870), https://www.law.cornell.edu/supremecourt/text/83/36 (accessed 12 May 2015), 27

De Souza v. Cobden [1891] 1 QB 687, 22

State of Iowa v. Walker 192 Iowa 823; 185 NW 619 (1921), 50

Taylor v. Louisiana 19 US 522 (1975), 51

Thatcher v. Penn., Ohio, & Detroit Rd Co. I33 Ohio App. 242, 168 NE 859 (1928), 50

Tremblay v. Daigle [1989] 2 SCR 530, 37

US v. Yazell 832 US 341 (1966), 85*n*14

Viscountess Rhondda's Claim [1922] 2 AC 339, 30, 49, 119

Walker v. Beamy, 36 Pa. State Rep. 410, 69*n*13

Waters and Jurek (1995) FLC ¶ 92–635, 67

Wellesley v. Wellesley [1828] 1 Dow. & Clark 481, 109, 114*n*15

Wellesley v. Wellesley (1829) 2 Russ. 3, 236, 109, 114*n*15

Wilkinson v. ASB Bank Ltd [1998] 1 NZLR 674, 85*n*16

Yerkey v. Jones [1939] HCA 3; (1939) 63 CLR 649 (6 March 1939), 76–7, 79–80, 85*n*7, 85*n*14–15, 85*n*18

DOI: 10.1057/9781137562357.0011

Bibliography

Sonya A. Adamo, 'The Injustice of the Marital Rape
    Exemption: A Survey of Common Law Countries',
    American University International Law Review, vol. 4, no.
    3, 1989, http://digitalcommons.wcl.american.edu/cgi/
    viewcontent.cgi?article=1613&context=auilr (accessed
    2 July 2015)

ALRC, *Equality before the Law*, ALRC 69, AGPS, Sydney,
    Australia, 1994

Brent W. Ambrose, Larry Cordell and Shuwei Ma, *The
    Impact of Student Loan Debt on Small Business Formation*,
    Social Science Research Network, 15 July 2015, http://
    papers.ssrn.com/sol3/papers.cfm?abstract_id=2417676
    (accessed 30 August 2015)

America's Historical Documents, *19th Amendment to
    the US Constitution*, 'Women's Right to Vote', http://
    www.archives.gov/historical-docs/document.
    html?doc=13&title.raw=19th+Amendment+to+the+U
    .S.+Constitution:+Women's+Right+to+Vote (accessed
    23 June 2015)

American Bar Association, *Magna Carta 800 – Foundation
    of Liberty – Events*, 2015, http://magnacarta800th.com/
    events/american-bar-association/ (accessed 13 July
    2015)

Anti-Discrimination Board, NSW, *Report*, NSW
    Government Printer, Sydney, Australia, 1987

The Aphra Behn Page, 2011, http://www.lit-arts.net/Behn/
    (accessed 4 July 2015)

Patricia Apps, *A Theory of Inequality and Taxation*, CUP,
    Cambridge, UK, 1981

DOI: 10.1057/9781137562357.0012

Archbold's Pleading and Evidence in Criminal Cases, 1822

Neill Atkinson, *Votes for Women – Te Ara Encyclopedia of New Zealand*, 2002, www.teara.govt.nz/en/voting-rights/page-4 (accessed 24 May 2015)

Australian Electoral Commission (AEC), *Electoral Milestones for Women*, http://www.aec.gov.au/elections/australian_electoral_history/milestone.htm (accessed 23 June 2015)

Australian Government, australia.gov.au, *Australian Women in Politics*, 2011, http://www.australia.gov.au/about-australia/australian-story/austn-women-in-politics (accessed 3 July 2015)

Australian Government, Department of Social Security, *Women in Australian Society – Milestones 1871—1983*, https://www.dss.gov.au/our-responsibilities/women/programs-services/research-and-data/women-in-australian-society-milestones-1871–1983#3 (accessed 15 May 2015)

Australian Government, National Archives of Australia, *Australia's Prime Ministers – Andrew Fisher*, http://primeministers.naa.gov.au/primeministers/fisher/ (accessed 23 June 2015)

Australian Government, National Archives of Australia, *Australia's Prime Ministers – Margaret Fisher*, http://primeministers.naa.gov.au/primeministers/fisher/spouse.aspx (accessed 23 June 2015)

Kate Auty and Sandy Toussaint (eds), *A Jury of Whose Peers? The Cultural Politics of Juries in Australia*, UWA Press, Crawley, Australia, 2004

AVAWA Secretariat, *Trust the Women*, http://timeline.awava.org.au/archives/202 (accessed 23 June 2015)

BBC, 'Abortion law change blocked in NI Assembly', 3 June 2015, http://www.bbc.co.uk/news/uk-northern-ireland-32987714 (accessed 5 June 2015)

BBC, 'Woman dies after abortion request "refused" at Galway hospital', 14 November 2012, http://www.bbc.co.uk/news/uk-northern-ireland-20321741 (accessed 5 June 2015)

BBC News, 'Suffragette Viscountess Rhondda's Newport bomb attack remembered', 2 June 2013, http://www.bbc.co.uk/news/uk-wales-22740340 (accessed 3 July 2015)

BBC News, 'Thailand bans commercial surrogacy', February 2015, http://www.bbc.co.uk/news/world-asia-31546717 (accessed 28 August 2015)

Constance Backhouse, 'Married Women's Property Law in Nineteenth-Century Canada', *Law and History Review*, vol. 6, no. 2, Autumn 1988, pp. 211–257, http://papers.ssrn.com/sol3/papers.cfm?abstract_id=2273326 (accessed 18 May 2015)

DOI: 10.1057/9781137562357.0012

QUH Der Balfour, *The Jury. A Handbook of Law and Procedure*, Butterworths, Toronto, Canada, 1998

Joel Barlow, *Advice to the Privileged Orders*, Joseph Johnson Publisher, London, UK, 1792; cited Lyndall Gordon, *Vindication – A Life of Mary Wollstonecraft*, Virago, London, 2005, p. 164

Angela Barns, Andrew Cowie and Therese Jefferson, *Women's Property Rights: A Herstorical Dialogue of Economic Thought and Gender Inequality*, WiSER, Curtin University, Perth, Australia, 2009

Felice Batlan, *Women and Justice for the Poor – A History of Legal Aid*, CUP, Cambridge, UK, 2015

Mary Ritter Beard, *Woman as Force in History – A Study in Traditions and Realities*, Collier, NY, USA, 1st edn, 1946; reprint Octagon Books, 1976

JM Beattie, *Crime and the Courts in England, 1660–1800*, PUP, Princeton, NJ, USA, 1986

Simone De Beauvoir, *The Second Sex*, Jonathan Cape, London, UK, 1953

Michael Beloff, 'Magna Carta in the Twentieth and Twenty First Centuries', *Denning Law Journal*, vol. 27, 2015, pp. 1–44

Judith M. Bennett and Ruth Mazo Karras, *The Oxford Handbook of Women and Gender in Medieval Europe*, OUP, Oxford, UK, 2013

Riva Berleant, 'Harriet Martineau (1802–1876)', 2005, http://www.brycchancarey.com/abolition/martineau.htm (accessed 22 June 2015)

Lois S. Bibbings, *Binding Men: Stories about Violence and Law in Late Victorian England*, Routledge, Oxford, UK, 2014

Greta Bird and Elizabeth Kirkby (ed.), *Sex, Power and Justice: Historical Perspectives on Law in Australia*, OUP, Melbourne, Australia, 1995

Michael Bittman, *Juggling Time: How Australian Families Use Their Time*, AGPS, Canberra, Australia, 1991

Blackstone's Commentaries on the Laws of England, vol. 1, 1765, 1793 edns

Barbara Leigh-Smith Bodichon, *Brief Summary, in Plain Language, of the Most Important Laws of England Concerning Women*, J. Chapman, London, UK, 1854, http://womhist.alexanderstreet.com/awrm/doc17.htm (accessed 31 August 2015)

Janette Bomford, *That Dangerous and Persuasive Woman: Vida Goldstein*, Melbourne University Press, Carlton, Australia, 1993

Owen Bowcott, 'No-fault divorces "should be standard"', *Guardian*, 27 March 2012, http://www.theguardian.com/law/2012/mar/27/no-fault-divorces-standard-judge (accessed 19 May 2015)

Bettina Bradbury (ed.), *Canadian Family History: Selected Readings*, Copp Clark Pitman, Toronto, Canada, 1992, pp. 320–359

DOI: 10.1057/9781137562357.0012

Paul Brand, ' "Deserving" and "Undeserving" Wives: Earning and Forfeiting Dower in Medieval England', *Journal of Legal History*, vol. 22, April 2001, pp. 1–20

Alison Brewin, *Legal Aid Denied: Women and the Cuts to Legal Services in BC*, CCPA & LEAF (Women's Legal Education & Action Fund), BC, Canada, 2004

Raymond Brooks, 'The Melbourne Tailoresses' Strike 1882–1883: An Assessment', *Labour History*, no. 44, 1983, pp. 27–38

Margaret Brown, 'Cowan, Edith Dircksey (1861–1932)' in *Australian Dictionary of Biography*, vol. 8, Melbourne University Press, Melbourne, Australia, 1981, http://adb.anu.edu.au/biography/cowan-edith-dircksey-5791 (accessed 3 July 2015)

Janice N. Brownfoot, 'Dugdale, Henrietta Augusta (1827–1918)', *Australian Dictionary of Biography*, vol. 4, 1992, http://adb.anu.edu.au/biography/dugdale-henrietta-augusta-3452 (accessed 21 June 2015)

Susan Brownmiller, *Against Our Will – Men, Women and Rape*, Martin Secker & Warburg, NY, USA, 1975

Sue Bruley, *Women in Britain since 1900*, Palgrave Macmillan, London, UK, 1999

Michael Bryan, 'The Great Inflation – 1965 – 1982', *Federal Reserve History*, 2013, http://www.federalreservehistory.org/Period/Essay/13 (accessed 15 May 2015).

Karen Buczynski-Lee, *When Mourning Becomes Electric*, VCA MA (Film), 2010, Victoria, Australia

Maureen Baker, *Families, Labour and Love*, UBC Press, Vancouver, Canada, 2001

Canadian Advisory Council on the Status of Women, *Canadian Charter Equality Rights for Women: One Step Forward or Two Steps Back?* CACSW, Montreal, Canada, 1989

David Carpenter, *Magna Carta*, Penguin Classics, London, 2015

Colin Cartwright, 'No vote, no tax – the Suffragettes and their tax protest', *Tax Justice Network*, 2011, http://taxjustice.blogspot.co.uk/2011/09/hammer-blows-of-tax-protest-suffragette.html (accessed 24 June 2015)

Catholic Encyclopedia, *St Elizabeth of Shonau*, http://www.newadvent.org/cathen/05392a.htm (accessed 3 July 2015)

Catholic Encyclopedia, *St Hildegard*, http://www.newadvent.org/cathen/07351a.htm (accessed 3 July 2015)

DOI: 10.1057/9781137562357.0012

Anne Lorene Chambers, *Married Women and Property Law in Victorian Ontario*, Osgoode Society for Canadian Legal History, UTP, Ontario, Canada, 1997

Michael Chesterman, 'OJ and the Dingo: how media publicity relating to criminal cases tried by jury is dealt with in Australia and America', *American Journal of Comparative Law*, vol. 45, no. 1, 1997, pp. 109–147

Helen M. Cam, *The Hundred and the Hundred Rolls: An Outline of Government in Medieval England*, 1930, 1963 new edn, Metheun & Co., London, UK, p. 137; online edn, https://www.questia.com/read/6669156/the-hundred-and-the-hundred-rolls-an-outline-of-local (accessed 14 May 2015)

Stephen Church, *King John – England, Magna Carta and the Making of a Tyrant*, Macmillan, London, UK, 2015

Richard Chused, 'Married Women's Property Law, 1800–1850', *Georgetown Law Journal*, vol 71, 1983, pp. 1359–1389

Daniel P. Cipollone, 'The liabilities of securities', *Western Journal of Legal Studies*, vol. 4, no. 2, 2014, http://ir.lib.uwo.ca/uwojls/vol4/iss2/2/ (accessed 23 June 2015)

Frances Power Cobbe, 'Wife torture in England', *Contemporary Review*, 1878; reprinted Jill Radford and Diana EH Russell (eds), *Femicide: The Politics of Woman Killing*, Open University Press, Buckingham, UK, 1992

Edward Coke, *Institutes of the Lawes of England*, Pts 1-1v, Flesher & Ors, London, UK, 1628–1644, http://www.constitution.org/Coke/Coke.htm

A Country By Consent, *World War I*, 'Women Get the Vote 1916–1919', http://www.canadahistoryproject.ca/1914/1914–08-women-vote.html (accessed 23 June 2015)

Lyn Craig and Pooja Sawrikar, 'Housework and divorce: the division of domestic labour and relationship breakdown in Australia', in *Relationship Survival*, Melbourne Institute, Australia, 2007, https://www.melbourneinstitute.com/downloads/hilda/Bibliography/HILDA_Conference_Papers/2007_papers/Sawrikar,%20Pooja_final%20paper.pdf (accessed 20 May 2015)

Shani D'Cruz, 'Women and the family', in June Purvis (ed.), *Women's History: Britain, 1850–1945 – An Introduction*, Routledge, Oxford, UK, 1995, pp. 51–84

Current Comment, 'Trial by a jury one's peers?' *Australian Law Journal*, vol. 56, 1982, pp. 209–210

DOI: 10.1057/9781137562357.0012

Shabnam Dastheib, ' "Rent-a-womb" babies could end up stateless', *The Dominion Post*, http://www.stuff.co.nz/national/health/5477716/Rent-a-womb-babies-could-end-up-stateless (accessed 28 August 2015)

Martha Craig Daughtrey, 'Women and the constitution: where we are at the end of the century', *New York University Law Review*, vol. 75, 2000, pp. 1–25

This Day in History, *31 March, American Revolution 1776 Abigail Adams urges husband to 'remember the ladies'*, http://www.history.com/this-day-in-history/abigail-adams-urges-husband-to-remember-the-ladies (accessed 5 July 2015)

This Day in History, *Old West – Wyoming Grants Women the Vote*, http://www.history.com/this-day-in-history/wyoming-grants-women-the-vote (accessed 27 May 2015)

Karen DeCrow, *Sexist Justice*, Random House, New York, USA, 1975

Joey L. Defrancesco and David Segal, 'Labour History: The First Factory Strike', 1 September 2014, http://inthesetimes.com/article/17050/the_mother_of_all_strikes (accessed 23 June 2015)

James Donovan, 'The retreat from Yerkey v. Jones: from status back to contract', *University of Western Australia Law Review*, vol. 26, 1996, pp. 309–331

Ciaran Doolin, 'They will never crush out the Union! The role of women in the 1890 maritime strike', *What She Said*, no. 2, http://fightback.org.nz/2014/07/01/they-will-never-crush-out-the-union-the-role-of-women-in-the-1890-maritime-strike/ (accessed 23 June 2015)

Emily Dugan, 'Revealed: surrogate births hit record high as couples flock abroad', *Independent on Sunday*, 20 March 2015, http://www.independent.co.uk/news/uk/home-news/revealed-surrogate-births-hit-record-high-as-couples-flock-abroad-9162834.html (accessed 26 August 2015)

Andrea Dworkin, *Pornography – Men Possessing Women*, The Women's Press, London, UK, 1981

Andrea Dworkin and Catharine A. Mackinnon, *In Harm's Way: The Pornography Civil Rights Hearings*, HUP, Cambridge, US, 1997

East's Treatise of the Pleas of the Crown, 1803

'Edith Thompson and Frederick Bywaters', *Capital Punishment*, http://www.capitalpunishmentuk.org/edith.html (accessed 14 June 2015)

Editorial, 'Melinda Leves' hard case', *Sydney Morning Herald*, 7 July 1986, p. 12, https://news.google.com/newspapers?nid=1301&dat=19860707

DOI: 10.1057/9781137562357.0012

&id=PjZWAAAAIBAJ&sjid=NegDAAAAIBAJ&pg=2121,4348329&hl
=en (accessed 23 June 2015)

Susan Edwards, *Female Sexuality and the Law*, Blackstone, London, UK, 1981

Susan Edwards, *Sex and Gender in the Legal Process*, Blackstone, London, UK, 1996, 4th edn 2013

The Elizabeth Cady Stanton and Susan B. Anthony Papers Project, *Sentiments and Resolutions – Women's Rights Convention, Held at Seneca Falls, 19–20 July 1948*, 'Seneca Falls Declaration', http://ecssba.rutgers.edu/docs/seneca.html (accessed 24 May 2015); published in Ann D. Gordon (ed.), *The Elizabeth Cady Stanton and Susan B. Anthony Papers Project*, RUP, New Brunswick, US, 1997

Elizabeth C. Wolstenholme Elmy, *A Collection of Pamphlets and Leaflets Relating to the Guardianship of Infants* (most written or published by ECW Elmy), publisher unknown, London, 1883.

EC Wolstenholme Elmy, *The Decision in the Clitheroe Case, and Its Consequences: A Series of Five Letters*, Guardian Print Works, Manchester, UK, 1891

Mary Louise Erickson, *Women and Property in Early Modern*, England, Routledge, Oxford, UK, 1993

Fawcett Society, *Sex and Power 2013: Who Runs Britain?* Fawcett Society, London, 2013

Eleanor Flexner, *Century of Struggle: The Women's Rights Movement in the United States*, 1959, reprint with update Ellen Fitzpatrick, Belknapp Press/HUP, Cambridge, USA, 1996

Hilary Frances, ' "Pay the piper, call the tune!" The Women's Tax Resistance League', in Maroula Joannou and June Purvis (eds), *The Women's Suffrage Movement: New Feminist Perspectives*, MUP, Manchester, UK, 1998, chapter 4, pp. 64–75

Felix Frankfurter, 'The Supreme Court in the Mirror of Justices', *Pennsylvania Law Review*, 1957, vol. 105, no. 6, pp. 781–795

'From Dot to Domesday', trns JA Giles, http://www.dot-domesday.me.uk/matwest.htm (accessed 28 May 2015)

Frances Dana Gage, 'Ain't I a Woman', http://www.sojournertruth.org/Library/Speeches/AintIAWoman.htm (accessed 3 July 2015)

Gilbert Geis and Ivan Bunn, *A Trial of Witches: A Seventeenth-century Witchcraft Prosecution*, Routledge, London, UK, 1997

DOI: 10.1057/9781137562357.0012

Gender Bias and the Law Project, *Heroines of Fortitude: The Experience of Women in Court as Victims of Sexual Assault,* Department for Women, NSW, Sydney, Australia, 1996

Joshua S. Getzler, 'Cresswell, Sir Cresswell [*formerly* Cresswell Easterby] (1793–1863), *Judge*', *Oxford Dictionary of National Biography*, Oxford University Press, Oxford, UK, 2004, online edn 2009, http://www.oxforddnb.com/view/article/6673 (accessed 18 May 2015).

Jessica A. Gibson, 'What Are You? – A Woman I Suppose': Women in the Eighteenth-Century British Court, MA Thesis, University of Oregon, 2013

James Giardner (ed.), *The Project Gutenberg EBook of The Paston Letters*, vol. I, http://www.gutenberg.org/files/43348/43348-h/43348-h.htm (accessed 3 July 2015)

Ranulf de Glanville, *Treatise on the Laws and Customs of the Kingdom of England*, 1780, Trns and Introduction, John Beale, John Byrne & Co, Washington, DC, USA, 1900, http://archive.org/stream/cu31924021674399/cu31924021674399_djvu.txt (accessed 24 May 2015)

'The Glory of a Pioneer', Ada Evans Chambers, Sydney, http://adaevanschambers.com/?page_id=2 (accessed 12 May 2015)

Vida Goldstein, *Woman Suffrage in Australia*, reprinted Victorian Women's Trust, Melbourne, Australia, 2008

Vida Goldstein, *To America and Back, January-July 1902: A Lecture by Vida Goldstein*, Prepared for publication by Jill Roe, Australian History Museum, Sydney, Australia, 2002

Lyndall Gordon, *Vindication – A Life of Mary Wollstonecraft*, Virago, London, 2005

Regina Graycar and Jenny Morgan, *The Hidden Gender of Law,* 2nd edn, Federation Press, Sydney, Australia 2002

Germaine Greer, *The Female Eunuch*, Paladin, London, UK, 1970

Hale's History of the Pleas of the Crown (or *Hale's Pleas of the Crown*), Nutt and Gosling, London, UK, 1736

Cicely Hamilton, *Marriage as a Trade*, Moffat, Yard & Company, New York, USA, 1909; reprinted 1971, https://archive.org/details/marriageasatradoohamigoog (accessed 25 August 2015)

June Hannam, 'Women and Politics', in June Purvis (ed.), *Women's History: Britain, 1850–1945 – An Introduction*, Routledge, Oxford, UK, pp. 217–245

DOI: 10.1057/9781137562357.0012

Valerie P. Hans and Neil Vidmar, *Judging the Jury*, Perseus Publishing, Cambridge, MA, USA, 1986

Karen Harris and Lori Caskey-Sigety, *The Medieval Vagina – A Hysterical and Historical Perspective of All Things Vaginal During the Middle Ages*, Snark Publishing, Indiana, USA, 2014

Heldris, *Silence: A Thirteenth-Century French Romance*, S. Roche-Mahdi (ed.), Colleagues Press, East Lansing, US, 1992

Leslie Henderson, *The Goldstein Story*, Stockland Press, Melbourne, Australia, 1973

Heritage Newfoundland and Labrador, *The Modern Women's Movement*, http://www.heritage.nf.ca/articles/politics/modern-women-movement.php (accessed 215 May 2015)

Herstoria, *Women's Access to Higher Education: An Overview (1860–1948)*, July 2012, http://herstoria.com/?p=535 (accessed 21 May 2015)

Ranulf Higden, *Polychronicon*, 14th century, https://archive.org/stream/polychroniconraoolumbgoog/polychroniconraoolumbgoog_djvu.txt (accessed 14 August 2015)

Catey Hill, '5 times it's more expensive to be a woman', *MW Market Watch*, 14 April 2015, http://www.marketwatch.com/story/5-things-women-pay-more-for-than-men-2014-01-17 (accessed 23 June 2015)

James F. Hodgson and Jennifer S. Kelley, *Sexual Violence: Policies, Practices and Challenges in the United States and Canada*, Praeger Publishers, Westport, US, 2002

Lee Holcombe, *Wives and Property: Reform of the Married Women's Property Law in Nineteenth Century England*, UTP, Ontario, Canada, 1983

William Holdsworth, 'Sir Matthew Hale', *Law Quarterly Review*, vol. 39, no. 4, 1923, p. 407

Kitty Holland, *Savita – The Tragedy that Shook a Nation*, Transworld Ireland/Random House, London, UK, 2013

Oliver Wendell Holmes, 'The Path of Law', *Harvard Law Review*, vol. 10, 1897; in *Collected Legal Papers*, Harcourt Brace & Howe, New York, USA, 1920; reprinted Peter Smith, New York, USA, 1952, https://archive.org/stream/collectedlegalpa027872mbp/collectedlegalpa027872mbp_djvu.txt (accessed 23 June 2015)

JC Holt, *Colonial England – 1066–1215*, Hambledon Press, London, UK, 1997

JC Holt, *Magna Carta*, revised edn, CUP, Cambridge, UK, 2015

DOI: 10.1057/9781137562357.0012

JC Holt, *The Northerners – A Study in the Reign of King John*, Clarendon Press, Oxford, UK, 1992

House of Lords, *Hansard*, vol. 58, 17 July 1924, p. 711

House of Lords, *Hansard*, vol. 61, 25 May 1925, p. 45

House of Representatives, No. 92–359, 92d Congress [1971]

Susan Jackel, *Women's Suffrage*, Historic Canada, 2013, http://www.thecanadianencyclopedia.ca/en/article/womens-suffrage/ (accessed 5 July 2015)

Edmund Jackson, *The True Story of the Clitheroe Abduction: Or Why I Rran Away with My Wife*, NE Lancashire Print & Publishing Co, Blackburn, UK, 1891 (HW Burnett, ed., currently out of print)

Emily Jackson, 'Vindication' *Lancashire Evening Post*, reprinted as 'The Clitheroe Case' etc *Times*, 18, 20, 21, 22, 23 April 1891

F. Tennyson Jesse, *A Pin to See the Peepshow*, Wm Heinemann, London, UK, 1934; Virago edn, London, UK, 1979

Sophia Jex-Blake, 'The medical education of women (1873)', in Dale Spender (ed.), *The Education Papers: Women's Quest for Equality in Britain 1850–1912*, Routledge & Kegan Paul, London, UK, 1987, pp. 268–276

A. John (ed.), *Unequal Opportunities: Women's Employment in England 1800–1918*, Blackwell, Oxford, UK, 1986

Claire Jones, 'The Married Women's Property Acts (UK, 1870, 1882 and 1893)' *Herstoria*, 7 July 2012, 19th Century, Articles, http://herstoria.com/?p=473 (accessed 19 May 2015)

FJE Jordan, 'The Federal Divorce Act (1968) and the Constitution', *McGill Law Journal*, vol. 14, no. 2, 1968, pp. 209–227, http://lawjournal.mcgill.ca/userfiles/other/386488-jordan.pdf (accessed 18 May 2015)

Robin Joyce, 'Feminism – An Early Tradition Amongst Western Australian Labor Women', in Women & Labour Conference Collective (eds), *All Her Labors – Working It Out*, vol. 1, Hale & Iremonger, Sydney, Australia, 1984, pp. 148–158

Robin Joyce, 'Labor Women – Political Housekeepers or Politicians?', in Marian Simms (ed.), *Australian Women and the Political System*, Longman Cheshire, Melbourne, Australia, 1986, pp. 66–76

Harry Kalven Jnr and Hans Zeisel, *The American Jury*, Little Brown & Co, Boston, MA, USA, 1966

Leo Kanowitz, *Women and the Law: The Unfinished Revolution*, NMU Press, Albuquerque, US, 1969

DOI: 10.1057/9781137562357.0012

Kristin (Brandser) Kasem, 'Looking for Law in All the Wrong Places: Outlaw Texts and Early Women's Advocacy', *Southern California Review of Law and Women's Studies*, vol. 13, 2003–2004, http://scholarship.law.uc.edu/cgi/viewcontent. cgi?article=1011&context=fac_pubs (accessed 23 June 2015)

Margery Kempe, *The Book of Margery Kempe*, Wynkyn de Worde, Fleet Street, London, UK, 1438, Annotated Edn, Barry Windeatt (ed.), Pearson Education Ltd & DS Brewer, Cambridge, UK, 2004

Helena Kennedy, *Eve Was Framed – Women and British Justice*, Vintage, London, 1993, 2005

Mary Keyes and Richard Chisholm, *Commercial Surrogacy – Some Troubling Family Law Issues*, flc-submission-professor-mary-keyes-griffith-university-16july2013 (accessed 21 August 2015)

John Maynard Keynes, *The General Theory of Employment, Interest and Money*, 1936, Macmillan, London, UK, 2007

Peter King, *Crime, Justice, and Discretion in England, 1740–1820*, OUP, Oxford, UK, 2000

Jennifer Kirby, 'These two Americans want babies through Indian surrogates: it hasn't been easy', *New Republic*, 10 December 2013, http://www.newrepublic.com/article/115873/fertility-tourism-seeking-surrogacy-india-thailand-mexico (accessed 23 June 2015)

Phyllis Korkky in 'The ripple effects of rising Student Debt' *New York Times*, 24 May 2014, http://www.nytimes.com/2014/05/25/business/the-ripple-effects-of-rising-student-debt.html?_r=0 (accessed 30 August 2015)

Jennifer Koshan, *The Legal Treatment of Marital Rape and Women's Equality: An Analysis of the Canadian Experience*, nd, http://theequalityeffect.org/pdfs/maritalrapecanadexperience.pdf (accessed 2 July 2015)

John Langbein, 'Shaping the eighteenth-century criminal trial: a view from the Ryder sources', *University of Chicago Law Review*, vol. 50, no. 1, 1983

Law Commission, *Women and Access to Justice*, Law Commission, Wellington, A/NZ, 1995–1999, http://www.lawcom.govt.nz/our-projects/women-and-access-justice (accessed 12 May 2015)

Law Commission, *Women's Access to Legal Services*, Law Commission, Wellington, A/NZ, 1999, http://www.lawcom.govt.nz/our-projects/women-and-access-justice (accessed 31 August 2015)

DOI: 10.1057/9781137562357.0012

Law Library of Congress, 'Married Women's Property Laws', http://
memory.loc.gov/ammem/awhhtml/awlaw3/property_law.html
(accessed 16 May 2015)

Law Reform Commission, Western Australia, *Selection, Eligibility and
Exemption of Jurors*, http://www.lrc.justice.wa.gov.au/_files/Ch01-
Jurors.pdf (accessed 31 August 2015)

Sarah Lawson, 'Introduction and notes' in Pizan, *The Treasure…*,
Penguin Books, London, UK, 1985, 2008, pp. iii–xxvii

Clara Lee, Letter to the Editor, *The Vote*, 6 July 1912

Beverly Lemire, *The Business of Everyday Life: Gender, Practice and Social
Politics in England c. 1600–1900*, MUP, Manchester, UK, 2005

Vicki Leon, *Outrageous Women of the Middle Ages*, John Wiley, New York,
NY, 1998

Jill Lepore, 'The rule of history – Magna Carta, the Bill of Rights, and
the hold of time', *New Yorker*, 20 April 2015, pp. 1–12, http://www.
newyorker.com/magazine/2015/04/20/the-rule-of-history (accessed 2
July 2015)

Henrietta Leyser, *Medieval Women – A Social History of Women in
England 450–1500*, Weidenfeld & Nicolson, London, 1995

Jill Liddington and Elizabeth Crawford, '"Women do not count,
neither shall they be counted": Suffrage, citizenship and the battle
for the 1911 Census', *History Workshop Journal*, vol. 1, 2011, http://
hwj.oxfordjournals.org/content/early/2011/02/21/hwj.dbq064.full
(accessed 24 May 2015)

Goran Lind, *Common Law Marriage: A Legal Institution for Cohabitation*,
OUP, New York, USA, 2008

Doug Linder, 'The Trial of Susan B. Anthony for illegal voting', 2001,
http://law2.umkc.ed/faculty/projects/ftrias/anthony/sbaacount.html
(accessed 21 May 2015)

www.parliament.uk, Living Heritage – Women and the Vote, 'Emily
Wilding Davison and Parliament', http://www.parliament.uk/about/
living-heritage/transformingsociety/electionsvoting/womenvote/
case-study-emily-wilding-davison/ewd/ (accessed 28 May 2015)

www.parliament.uk, Living Heritage – Women and the Vote,
'Petitions', http://www.parliament.uk/about/living-heritage/
transformingsociety/electionsvoting/womenvote/overview/petitions/
(accessed 24 June 2015)

www.parliament.uk, Living Heritage – Women and the Vote, 'Women
Get the Vote', http://www.parliament.uk/about/living-heritage/

DOI: 10.1057/9781137562357.0012

transformingsociety/electionsvoting/womenvote/overview/thevote/ (accessed 23 June 2015)

www.parliament.uk, Living Heritage ... ; 1911Census.co.uk, *About the 1911 Census*, 'The 1911 census and the suffragettes', http://www.1911census. co.uk/Content/default.aspx?r=24 (accessed 28 May 2015)

Kathryn Jean Lopez and Kathleen Sloan, 'A War on Women that Left and Right Can End Together', NR Interview, *National Review*, 28 June 2013, http://www.nationalreview.com/article/352254/wombs-rent-interview (accessed 23 June 2015)

Enid Lyons, *Among the Carrion Crows*, Lansdowne Press, Melbourne, Australia, 1997

Catharine A. Mackinnon, *Are Women Human? And Other International Dialogues*, Belknap Press/HUP, Cambridge, USA, 2007

Catharine A. Mackinnon, *Toward a Feminist Theory of the State*, HUP, Cambridge, USA, 1989

Holly J. McCammon, *The U.S. Women's Jury Movements and Strategic Adaptation – A More Just Verdict*, CUP, Cambridge, UK, 2012

Elizabeth McDonald and Yvette Tinsley (eds), *From 'Real Rape' to Real Justice: Prosecuting Rape in New Zealand*, VUP, Wellington, New Zealand, 2011

Henry McDonald, 'Northern Ireland high court grants judicial review of abortion law', *Guardian*, 2 February 2015, http://www.theguardian. com/world/2015/feb/02/northern-ireland-high-court-hears-abortion-challenge-rape-incest (accessed 5 June 2015)

Alexander H. McLintock, *An Encyclopaedia of New Zealand*, Government Printer, Wellington, Aotearoa/New Zealand, 1966, http://www.teara. govt.nz/en/1966/family-homes (accessed 28 May 2015)

Manitoba – Digital Resources on Manitoba's History, 'Women Win the Vote', http://manitobia.ca/content/en/themes/wwv (accessed 23 June 2015)

Harriet Martineau, *Illustrations of Political Economy*, 9 vols, Charles Fox, London, UK, 1832–1834; Riva Berleant, 'Harriet Martineau (1802–1876)', http://www.brycchancarey.com/abolition/martineau. htm (accessed 22 June 2015)

Clare Midgley, 'Ethnicity, "race" and empire', in June Purvis (ed.), *Women's History: Britain, 1850–1945 – An Introduction*, Routledge, London, UK, 1995, pp. 247–276

DOI: 10.1057/9781137562357.0012

John Stuart Mill, *The Subjection of Women*, 1869, reprinted *On Liberty and The Subjection of Women*, Alan Ryan (ed.), Penguin Classics, London, UK, 2006

Dora Montefiore, *From a Victorian to a Modern*, E. Archer, London, UK, 1925, Chapter VI, 'Women Must Vote for the Laws They Obey and the Taxes They Pay', trns Ted Crawford, https://www.marxists.org/archive/montefiore/1925/autobiography/index.htm (accessed 24 May 2015)

Ian Mortimer, *The Time Traveller's Guide to Medieval England*, Vintage Books, London, 2009

Mary Jane Mossman, 'Feminism and Legal Method: The Difference It Makes', *Australian Journal of Law and Society*, vol. 3, 1986, pp. 30–42

Mary Jane Mossman, *The First Woman Lawyers: A Comparative Study of Gender, Law and the Legal Professions*, Hart Publishing, Portland, Canada, 2006

Janel Mueller, *The Early Modern Englishwoman: A Facsimile Library of Essential Works Pt 1: Printed Writings 1500–1640*, vol. 3, Scolar Press, Surrey, UK, 1997

Ann Mumford, *Tax Policy, Women and the Law – UK and Comparative Perspectives*, CUP, Cambridge, UK, 2010

National Library of Australia, *Trove*, 'Tailoresses Association of Melbourne (1882–1907)', http://trove.nla.gov.au/people/764052?c=people (accessed 23 June 2015)

Jessica A. Nelson, 'Isabella, Countess of Norfolk', *Women of Magna Carta*, http://magnacarta800th.com/schools/biographies/women-of-magna-carta/isabella-princess-of-scotland-and-countess-of-norfolk/ (accessed 28 August 2015)

news.com.au, 'Babies – thousands of infertile Australians paying for surrogacy in India and Thailand', *Latest in Lifestyle – Parenting*, 3 April 2014, http://www.news.com.au/lifestyle/parenting/thousands-of-infertile-australians-paying-for-surrogacy-in-india-and-thailand/story-fneto8xa-1226872653386 (accessed 23 June 2015)

Virginia Blomer Nordby, 'Rape Law Reform: the Michigan experience', in Scutt (ed.), *Rape Law Reform*, AIC, Canberra, ACT, Australia, 1980, pp. 3–36, http://www.aic.gov.au/media_library/archive/events-other/rape-law-reform.pdf (accessed 2 July 2015)

Northwest Territories HRC, *Celebrating 100 Years of Advancements – Human Rights and Women in Canada 1911–2011*, http://www.statusofwomen.nt.ca/pdf/Conference/presentations/Therese%20-%20Chronology%20of%20Human%20Rights%20for%20Women%201911.pdf (accessed 20 August 2015)

DOI: 10.1057/9781137562357.0012

Caroline Sheridan Norton, *The Separation of Mother and Child by the Law of 'Custody of Infants', Considered*, Roake and Varty, London, UK, 1838; reprinted Leopold Classic Library, Marston Gate, UK, nd

Wallace Notestein, *A History of Witchcraft in England from 1558 to 1718*, Kessinger Publishing Co, Whitefish, MT, USA, 2003

Official Reports 5th Series Parliamentary Debates: Commons, Vol. xxxvi (25 March–12 April 1912), cols 615–732

Inae Oh, 'Meryl Streep Is Pushing Congress to Finally Revive the Equal Rights Amendment', *Mother Jones*, 24 June 2015, http://www. motherjones.com/mixed-media/2015/06/meryl-streep-congress-equal-rights-amendment (accessed 25 June 2015)

Audrey Oldfield, *Australian Woman Suffrage*, CUP, Melbourne, Australia, 1993

Deidre Palk, *Gender, Crime, and Judicial Discretion, 1780–1830*, Royal Historical Society/Boydell, Woodbridge, UK, 2006

Patrick Parkinson, 'Quantifying the Homemaker Contribution in Family Property Law', [2003] FedLawRev 1; vol. 31, no. 1, *Federal Law Review*, 2003, pp. 1–13, http://www.austlii.edu.au/au/journals/ FedLRev/2003/1.html (accessed 20 May 2015)

Parliament of Victoria, *Women's Suffrage Petition*, http://www.parliament. vic.gov.au/about/the-history-of-parliament/womens-suffrage-petition (accessed 23 June 2015)

The Paston Letters, vol. I, pp. 664–666; cited Henrietta Leyeser, *Medieval Women*, 1995, p. 167

Coventry Patmore, 'Husband and Wife – 1', *The Angel in the House*, Cassell & Company edn (David Price), London, UK, 1891, http://www. gutenberg.org/files/4099/4099-h/4099-h.htm (accessed 16 May 2015)

Joan Perkin, *Victorian Women*, NYU Press, NY, USA, 1995

Joan Perkin, *Women and Marriage in Nineteenth Century England*, Routledge, London UK, 1989

Roderick Phillips, *Divorce in New Zealand: A Social History*, OUP, Auckland, Aotearoa/New Zealand, 1981

Thomas Piketty, *Capital in the Twenty-First Century*, 2013, trns Arthur Goldhammer, Harvard College, Harvard, USA, 2014

Christine De Pizan, *The Book of the City of Ladies*, 1405, Penguin Classics edn, London, UK, 1999, Rosalind Brown-Grant Trns, 'Introduction'

Christine De Pizan, *The Treasure of the City of Ladies*, 1405, Penguin Classics edn, Penguin Books, London, UK, 1985, 2008

DOI: 10.1057/9781137562357.0012

Erin Pizzey, *Scream Quietly Or the Neighbours Will Hear*, Pelican, Harmondsworth, UK, 1974

Sir Frederick Pollock and Frederick William Maitland, *History of English Law Before the Time of Edward I*, 1895, reprint CUP, Cambridge, UK, 1968

Eileen Power, *Medieval Women*, MM Postan, ed, CUP, Cambridge, UK, 1995

Eileen Power, *Medieval English Nunneries c. 1275 to 1535*, CUP, Cambridge, 1922

Rebecca Probert, *Family Law in England and Wales*, Kluwer Law International, The Netherlands, 2011

Rebecca Probert, 'The Myths of History', *Modern Marriage Conference – Myths, Realities and Prospects*, 2013, http://www.marriagefoundation. org.uk/Web/Content/Default.aspx?Content=434 (accessed 18 May 2015)

Pro-Choice Action Network, 1999, http://www.prochoiceactionnetwork-canada.org/articles/canada.shtml (accessed 12 May 2015)

Jill Radford and Diana EH Russell (eds), *Femicide: The Politics of Woman Killing*, Open University Press, Buckingham. UK, 1992

Heather Radi, 'Whose child', in Judy Mackinolty and Heather Radi (eds), *In Pursuit of Justice – Australian Women & the Law 1788–1979*, Allen & Unwin, Sydney, Australia, 1979

Ranulf (Ranulph) Higden's Polychronicon, Polychronicon Ranulphi Higden monachi Cestrensis; together with English translations of John Trevisa and an unknown writer of the fifteenth century, https://archive.org/stream/polychroniconraoolumbgoog/ polychroniconraoolumbgoog_djvu.txt (accessed 28 May 2015)

Register of Rich Widows and of Orphaned Heirs and Heiresses, 1185, referenced Leyser, *Medieval Women*, 1995, pp. 87, 171

Elizabeth Reis, *Damned Witches: Sinners and Witches in Puritan New England*, CU Press, Ithaca, NY, USA, 1997

Deborah L. Rhode, *Access to Justice*, OUP, NY, USA, 2002

Rights of Women, *Access to Justice: A Report on Women's Access to Free Legal Advice in Hackney, Haringey, Lambeth and Tower Hamlets*, Rights of Women, London, UK, 2002

Julian V. Roberts and Robert J. Gebotys, 'Reporting rape laws: effects of legislative cChange in Canada', *Law and Human Behaviour*, vol. 16, no. 5, 1995, pp. 555–573

DOI: 10.1057/9781137562357.0012

Albie Sachs and Joan Hoff Wilson, *Sexism and the Law – A Study of Male Beliefs and Judicial Bias*, Martin Robinson, Oxford, UK, 1978

Marylynn Salmon, *Women and the Law of Property in Early America*, University of Nth Carolina Press, Carolina, USA, 1986

Marian Sawer and Gail Radford, *Making Women Count – A History of the Women's Electoral Lobby in Australia*, UNSW Press, Sydney, Australia, 2008

Simon Schama, *Rough Crossings: Britain, the Slaves and the American Revolution*, HarperCollins Publishers, New York, US, 2006

Regina Schuller and Neil Vidmar, 'The Canadian Criminal Jury', *Chicago-Kent Law* Review, vol. 86, no. 2, 2011, pp. 497–435

Jocelynne A. Scutt, 'Achieving the "impossible": women, girls and equal rights in education', in Scutt, *The Sexual Gerrymander*, 1994, pp. 219–237

Jocelynne A. Scutt, 'Cash or kind: economic violence and sexually transmitted debt', in Aysan Sev'er (ed.), *A Cross-Cultural Exploration of Wife Abuse: Problems and* Prospects, Edwin Mellen, New Jersey, US, 1997, pp. 145–172

Jocelynne A. Scutt, 'Consent in rape: the problem of the marriage contract', *Monash University Law Review*, 1977, vol. 3, no. 4, pp. 277–298

Jocelynne A. Scutt, *Rape Law Reform*, AIC, Canberra, Australia, 1980

Jocelynne A. Scutt, *Even in the Best of Homes – Violence in the Family*, Pelican Australia, Melbourne, Australia, 1983, McCulloch Publishing, Melbourne, Australia, 1990

Jocelynne A. Scutt, 'Fair Shares of Our Heritage: Women, Men and the Socialist Ideal' in Scutt, *The Sexual Gerrymander*, 1994, pp. 18–37

Jocelynne A. Scutt, *The Incredible Woman – Power & Sexual Politics*, 2 vols, Artemis Publishing, Melbourne, Australia, 1996

Jocelynne A. Scutt (ed), *Living Generously – Women Mentoring Women*, Artemis Publishing, Melbourne, Australia, 1996

Jocelynne A. Scutt, 'Murphy and Family Law', in Scutt (ed.), *Lionel Murphy – A Radical Judge*, McCulloch-Macmillan, Melbourne, Australia, 1986

Jocelynne A. Scutt, 'Police, prosecution, courts and wartime demonstrations: Adela Pankhurst in the Australian High Court', *Denning Law Journal*, vol. 23, no. 1, 2011, pp. 65–91

Jocelynne A. Scutt, *The Sexual Gerrymander – Women and the Economics of Power*, Spinifex Press, Melbourne, Australia, 1994

DOI: 10.1057/9781137562357.0012

Jocelynne A. Scutt (ed.), *Singular Women – Reclaiming Spinsterhood*, Artemis Publishing, Melbourne, Victoria, 1994

Jocelynne A. Scutt, Wage Rage – The Long, Long Struggle for Equal Pay, PhD Thesis, University of New South Wales, 2007

Jocelynne A. Scutt, *Women and the Law*, Law Book/Thomson, Sydney, Australia, 1990

Jocelynne A. Scutt and Di Graham, *For Richer, For Poorer – Money, Marriage and Property Rights*, Penguin Books, Melbourne, Australia, 1984

Jane Sendall, *Family Law Handbook*, OUP, Oxford, UK, 2015

Mary Lyndon Shanley, *Feminism, Marriage, and the Law in Victorian England 1850–1895*, Princeton University Press, Princeton, USA, 1989

James Sharpe, 'Hopkins, Matthew (d. 1647)', *Dictionary of National Biography*, OUP, Oxford, UK, 2004

Robert J. Sharpe and Patricia I. McMahon, *The Persons Case – The Origins and Legacy of the Fight for Legal Personhood*, UTP, Ontario, Canada, 2007

Walter Simons, *Cities of Ladies: Beguine Communities in the Medieval Low Countries, 1200–1565*, UP Press, Philadelphia, USA, 2001

Leigh Simpkin, 'Rape Law Reform (No. 2) Act 1985', *Auckland University Law Review*, vol. 5, no. 4, 1987, pp. 514–519

Lis Smith, 'A woman is a person! Sophia Jex-Blake's historical struggle', WHN Blog, 22 March 2012, http://womenshistorynetwork.org/blog/?p-1096 (accessed 22 May 2015)

Harold L. Smith, *Women's Suffrage Campaign 1866–1928*, Longman, London, UK, 1998, revised edn, 2007

Dale Spender (ed.), *The Education Papers: Women's Quest for Equality in Britain 1850–1912*, Routledge & Kegan Paul, London, UK, 1987

Dale Spender, *Women of Ideas and What Men Have Done to Them*, revised edn, HarperCollins Publishers, Canada, 1990

Stanford Encyclopaedia of Philosophy, *Mary Astell*, 2005, http://plato.stanford.edu/entries/astell/ (accessed 3 July 2015)

Elizabeth Cady Stanton, *Women's Bible*, Parts I & II, 1895, 1898, http://lcweb2.loc.gov/cgi-bin/query/r?ammem/mcc:@field(DOCID+@lit(mcc/049)) (accessed 31 August 2015)

David Starke, *Magna Carta – The True Story behind the Charter*, Hodder & Stoughton, London, 2015

Susan Staves, *Married Women's Separate Property in England, 1660–1833*, HUP, Cambridge, US, 1990

Stephen's Digest of the Criminal Law, 1877 edn

DOI: 10.1057/9781137562357.0012

Charlotte Carmichael Stopes, *British Freewomen: Their Historical Privilege,* 1894, 1907 3rd edn reprint, CUP, Cambridge, UK, 2010

Surrogacy in Canada OnLine, 'Cost of Surrogacy', http://www.surrogacy.ca/services/the-cost-of-surrogacy.html (accessed 28 August 2015)

Laura Swan, *The Wisdom of the Beguines: The Forgotten Story of a Medieval Women's Movement,* Bluebridge, Katona, NY, 2014

Norman P. Tanner, *The Church in Late Medieval Norwich, 1370–1532,* Pontifical Institute of Medieval Studies, Toronto, Canada, 1984

Harriet Taylor Mill, 'Enfranchisement of Women', *Westminster Review,* vol. 55, 1851, pp. 295–296; reprinted Ann P. Robson and John M. Robson (eds), *Sexual Equality: Writings by John Stuart Mill, Harriet Taylor Mill, and Helen Taylor,* UTP, Ontario, Canada, 1994, pp. 178–203

Marcelle Theibaux, *The Writings of Medieval Women: An Anthology,* 2nd edn, Routledge, London, UK, 1994

Margaret Thornton, *Dissonance and Distrust: Women and the Legal Profession,* OUP, Melbourne, Australia, 1996

Judith Treas and Sonja Drobnic (eds), *Dividing the Domestic: Men, Women, and Household Work in Cross-National Perspective,* Stanford University Press, California, US, 2010

A Tryal of Witches at the Assizes Held at Bury St Edmunds, William Shrewsbury, London, UK, 1682

United States House of Representatives – History, Art & Archives, *House of Representatives, Origins & Development: From the Constitution to Modern House – House of Representatives,* http://history.house.gov/Institution/Origins-Development/Proportional-Representation/ (accessed 4 July 2015)

University of St Andrews, 'Dr No', Thursday 8 March 2012, http://www.st-andrews.ac.uk/news/archive/2012/title,82785,en.php (accessed 22 May 2015)

Neil Vidmar, *World Jury Systems,* OUP, Oxford, UK, 2000

Marilyn Wearing, *If Women Counted: A New Feminist Economics,* Harper & Row, NY, USA, 1988, republished as *Counting for Nothing – What Men Value and What Women are Worth,* MacMillan, Allen & Unwin, UTP, Ontario, 1991

D. Kelly Weisberg, 'Barred from the bar: women and legal education in the United States 1870–1890', *Journal of Legal Education,* vol. 28, 1977, pp. 485–507, http://repository.uchastings.edu/cgi/viewcontent.cgi?article=1781&context=faculty_scholarship (accessed 12 May 2015)

DOI: 10.1057/9781137562357.0012

Mary Welstead and Susan Edwards, *Family* Law, 4th edn, OUP, Oxford, UK, 2013

Louise Wilkinson, 'Women as sheriffs in early thirteenth-century England', in Adrian Jobson (ed.), *English Government in the Thirteenth Century*, Boydell and Brewer, London, UK, 2004, pp. 111–124

Louise Wilkinson, 'Isabella of Angouleme, wife of King John', *Women of Magna Carta*, http://magnacarta800th.com/schools/biographies/women-of-magna-carta/isabella-of-angouleme-wife-of-king-john/ (accessed 28 August 2015)

Louise Wilkinson, 'Isabella, first wife of King John (d. 1217)', *Women of Magna Carta*, http://magnacarta800th.com/schools/biographies/women-of-magna-carta/isabella-of-gloucester/ (accessed 28 August 2015)

Louise Wilkinson, 'Joan, daughter of King John and wife of Llywelyn the Great (d. 1237)', *Women of Magna Carta*, http://magnacarta800th.com/schools/biographies/women-of-magna-carta/joan/ (accessed 28 August 2015)

Louise Wilkinson, 'Lady Nicholaa de la Haye (b. before 1169 – d. 1230)', *Magna Carta – Foundation of Liberty*, http://magnacarta800th.com/schools/biographies/women-of-magna-carta/lady-nicholaa-de-la-haye/ (accessed 2 July 2015)

Louise Wilkinson, 'Margaret, princess of Scotland', *Women of Magna Carta*, http://magnacarta800th.com/schools/biographies/women-of-magna-carta/margaret-princess-of-scotland-and-countess-of-kent/ (accessed 28 August 2015)

Joan Hoff Wilson, *Law, Gender, and Injustice: A Legal History of U.S. Women*, NYU Press, New York, USA, 1991

John Wilson, 'Nation and government – the legal system', *Te Ara – Encyclopedia of New Zealand*, updated 24-Mar-15, http://www.teara.govt.nz/en/document/2549/first-woman-on-a-jury (accessed 15 May 2015)

Helena Wojtczak, *British Women's Emancipation since the Renaissance – The 1868 Registration Battles*, 2009, http://www.historyofwomen.org/registration.html (accessed 22 May 2015)

Mary Wollstonecraft, *A Vindication of the Rights of Woman*, 1792, reprinted Penguin Books, London, England, 1999, 2004

A Woman Correspondent, 'The woman juror's new sphere', *Manchester Guardian*, 12 January 1921, reprinted *Guardian*, http://www.

DOI: 10.1057/9781137562357.0012

theguardian.com/theguardian/2011/jan/12/archive-the-woman-jurors-new-sphere-1921 (accessed 12 May 2015)

'Woman Juror – First to be Called – Service in Supreme Court', *Auckland Star*, 15 October 1943, p. 5

'Women and the Bar', *Spectator*, 12 December 1903, http://archive.spectator.co.uk/article/12th-december-1903/8/women-and-the-bar (accessed 12 May 2015)

Women's Political Association, *The Life and Work of Miss Vida Goldstein*, Australasian Authors' Agency, Melbourne, Australia, 1913

Pip Wright and Joy Wright, *Witches in and around Suffolk*, Pawprint Publishing, Stowmarket, UK, 2005

www.ourdocuments.gov, *One Hundred Milestone Documents*, '19th Amendment to the US Constitution: Women's Right to Vote (1920)', http://www.ourdocuments.gov/doc.php?flash=true&doc=63 (accessed 23 June 2015)

www.parliament.uk, *1913 Cat and Mouse Act (Prisoners (Temporary Discharge for Ill-Health) Act 1913*, http://www.parliament.uk/about/living-heritage/transformingsociety/electionsvoting/womenvote/case-study-the-right-to-vote/the-right-to-vote/winson-green-forcefeeding/cat-and-mouse-act/ (accessed 21 June 2015)

Filson Young, *Trial of Frederick Bywaters and Edith Thompson*, Notable British Trials Series, William Hodge & Company, London, UK, 1923; Law Book Company, Toronto, Canada, 1923; facsimile Notable British Trials Series, http://archive.org/stream/trialoffrederick015894mbp/trialoffrederick015894mbp_djvu.txt (accessed 14 May 2015)

Meta Zimmeck, 'Jobs for the girl: the expansion of clerical work for women 1850–1914', in A. John (ed.), *Unequal Opportunities: Women's Employment in England 1800–1918*, Blackwell, Oxford, UK, 1986

DOI: 10.1057/9781137562357.0012

Index

DOI: 10.1057/9781137562357.0013

WEL (Women's Electoral Lobby)
  Probate Action Group, 60
Whitehead, Mary Beth, 34
Wilkinson, Louise, 3, 10
Wilks, Elizabeth, 91
Wilks, Mark, 91
Williamson, Louise, 3, 10
Wilson, Joan Hoff, 6
Witchcraft Act 1542, 46, 47
witch trials, 46–7
Wojtczak, Helena, 19
Wollstonecraft, Mary, 4, 6, 10, 17, 60–1,
  73, 84, 117
women
  agency, 34–5
  bodily integrity, 9, 37–8, 112, 123
  campaign against taxation, 87, 91
  Census of 1911, 87–8
  Declaration of Independence, 88–9
  education, 23–7
  Equal Rights Amendment, 122–3
  freedom, 2, 4, 17, 45, 66, 73, 87–8,
    111–12, 121–2
  guarantors, 75–8, 80
  habeas corpus, 104, 106, 109–10
  jury duty, 48–51
  jury of her peers, 44–8
  lacking personhood, 33–8
  law and history, 4–10
  lawful judgment of peers, 51–3
  Magna Carta, 4–10
  marriage and Magna Carta, 67–8
  persons, 14–17

property ownership in marriage,
  57–60
rights and Magna Carta, 10–11
signing documents, 74–9
surrogacy, 34–5, 37
Women's Legal Status Act 1918, 33
women's rights
  abortion, 34–8
  activism, 16
  bodies of wives, 102–5
  contribution in marriage, 64–7
  custody of children, 98, 104
  equal pay, 96–9
  Equal Rights Amendment, 122–3
  husbands and equality, 79–81
  income, 74
  Magna Carta, 4, 8, 10–11, 116–17,
    120–1
  property ownership, 60–4, 74, 87, 89
  remedy, 81–4
  signing documents, 74–9
  taxation, 87–8
  voting, 21, 88, 92–6, 118, 122–3
Women's Suffrage Petition, 92
Women's Tax Resistance League, 89, 91
Wright, Anne, 47

Yerkey v. Jones (1939), 76–7, 79–80,
  127
Young, Filson, 41–2
Young, Warren, 7

Zeisel, Hans, 52

DOI: 10.1057/9781137562357.0013

Lightning Source UK Ltd.
Milton Keynes UK
UKOW04n0033300118
317051UK00007B/275/P